A Book Every Parent Should Read

HOW TO KEEP YOUR CHILDREN SAFE

A Book Every Parent Should Read

HOW TO KEEP YOUR CHILDREN SAFE
*Including Corona Virus Safety

Michael C. Bruno

DEDICATION

This book is dedicated to my wife Kathy for her amazing love and prayers, to our children, their spouses, and our grandchildren who continually light up our lives and to you as parents who are doing all that you can to ensure the safety and development of your children.

Special Thanks

Special thanks to Robin Ace for her typing, editing, and hard work to help make this book possible.

CONTENTS

Introduction Pg. 1

Chapter 1   Making the Main thing, the Main thing   Pg. 3-5

Chapter 2 Primary Areas of Harm   Pg. 6-18

Chapter 3 Parental Attributes   Pg. 19-39

Chapter 4 Twenty-Nine Wisdom Keys of Prevention   Pg. 40-91

Chapter 5 True Stories   Pg. 92-115

Chapter 6 Increasing the Odds   Pg. 116-122

Chapter 7 Predictive Analytics   Pg. 123-142

Chapter 8 You   Pg. 143-153

Chapter 9 Love   Pg. 154-168

Chapter 10 Corona Virus   Pg. 169-182

Chapter 11 Composite   Pg. 183-198

Chapter 12 A New Day   Pg. 199-216

Chapter 13 Confidence   Pg. 217-221

Chapter 14 Life is to be Good   Pg. 222-227

Evaluations & Babysitting Application   Pg. 228-235

About the Author   Pg. 236

Preface

Michael Bruno is the founder and director of Abba Ministries Counseling Center.

The primary focus of the center is to help prevent the abuse of children and to help those who have been victimized by abuse. For over 35 years, Michael Bruno has been an advocate for the safety of our children.

In today's society, the necessity of making the safety of our children our first priority is essential. In the following pages, you will be given specific tools to help you become more proficient regarding your own parenting skills regarding safety.

As well, I believe that this text will instill in all those who read it a passion to engage proactively in ensuring a society whose foundation is not only freedom, but the protection of all its people, especially its children.

AMCC Website: www.abbaministriescounselingcenter.com

AMCC E-mail: abbaministriescounselingcenter@yahoo.com

AMCC Address: 249 Grove City Road
Slippery Rock, Pa 1605

Introduction

In today's society, we are seeing things that have not been seen before. From sexual abuse scenarios and school shootings to bullying and an opioid epidemic, there are certainly great challenges in regard to parenting.

Due to directing a counseling center for almost 4 decades, I have seen up front what both children in today's society and parents are dealing with.Much of this text has come about through real life situations where real life solutions had to be realized.

This has translated into our sexual abuse program having a 95% success rate. It has translated into our program regarding victims of bullying recovering with total closure at a similar rate. Our work dealing with those with depression and suicidal predisposition has been very successful too.

As well, prevention has been of equal importance. It is great when someone who has been sexually abuse or bullied or harmed through a perpetrator on the internet receives healing and closure. It is obviously significantly better when the destructive situation is adverted altogether.

I cannot emphasize enough the motivation for this text and the proven solutions that will enable your children to be safe in an increasingly unsafe world.

No one knows fully the profound pain of abuse, addiction, depression, and victimization from shootings and abductions. It is imperative that we deal with the root causes of harm so that pain is nullified in the lives of our children.

How to Keep Your Children Safe

Chapter 1

Making the Main Thing, the Main Thing

I applaud all of you who are investing your time in reading this manuscript for the sake of your children or for children in general. Wisdom entails two main variables. The first is knowing what to make a priority in your life. The second is learning how to be successful in that which you do make a priority.

In essence, the first key is simply making the main thing, the main thing. For example, parents spend hundreds of hours in trying to find the appropriate college for their child. They thoroughly investigate the school's rating regarding the major of their student. They make visits to numerous universities and are willing to invest six figure tuition payments over four years.

However, amazingly when their child calls home and says that they are pledging a fraternity or sorority, many good parents almost nonchalantly say fine. As with most things, fraternities and sororities can be good or bad. A parent needs to find out about the specific frat or sorority their children are getting involved in. The following questions need to be asked. What is the average grade point average of the students in the frat or sorority? Have they ever been on probation? Are they known for partying or not? What are their hazing procedures, has anyone ever been harmed through the hazing activities?

The answers to these questions and you proactively communicating with your student can mean the difference between a beneficial or a very harmful college experience. So many parents that I have counseled after harm has taken place say that they only wished that they had known prior. Do not wish, be wise and know beforehand unto helping your child make right decisions.

I know that is strong. However, you have to understand that I have been dealing in the area of safety for almost 40 years. I have seen many children who have been spared harm and those who have been harmed. Accordingly, I have written this text through many tears. This includes tears of pain remembering scenarios of harm. It also includes tears of joy in the context of parents who have seen the truth due to wisdom prior to harm being realized.

There truly is no substitute for wisdom. Again, it enables one to prioritize correctly and to be successful in your areas of endeavor. Herein, I again commend you for making the safety of your children a primary priority. Safety obviously involves a commitment to protect those of a young age. However, it also involves children of all ages. In every age bracket, children need the support and encouragement of parents.

Knowledge

Knowledge is incredibly important. Ignorance is certainly not bliss. You can never deal with a situation when you are unaware of its existence. Likewise, you cannot successfully deal with a problem without the knowledge of the provision that is needed to be applied to it. In the following pages, both of these variables of knowledge will be conveyed.

Understanding

As well, with every aspect of knowledge shared, understanding will be conveyed. There is a tremendous difference between knowledge and understanding. Knowledge gives you the black and white facts regarding the challenges your child will face and specific answers in how to meet those challenges.

However, understanding goes much further. It is deeper. I can and will tell you specifics regarding challenges and age specific prevention strategies. However, all children have specific strengths and weaknesses. Good kids, really good kids can struggle in certain areas due to various variables of predisposition. Very simply, it is imperative that you know how to understand your child in his or her uniqueness.

The amazing thing about parenting is that it is not just doing the right things. It is how we do them. When a child is told the right thing to do and how to do it, it will help him immeasurably. When he understands you are telling him this in love and that you understand him or her, it will not only promote safety in its strongest fashion, it will realize relationship that every child is longing for.

Chapter 2

Primary Areas of Harm

It is imperative that we know specifically what we are up against. We will never gain victory over the enemy until we can properly identify who the enemy is. Herein, in the context of prevalence in American society, the primary areas of harm that your family will face are listed. It is important to note that this list is not in any way meant to bring fear to you, it is to do exactly the opposite. It is to empower you through the knowledge of that which you will face.

It is a different world than just 5 years ago. If I was not in the counseling field, I would certainly not be aware of the challenges our children are facing and to what degree. Let us now look at the specific areas of challenge.

<u>Sexual Abuse</u>

Statistics emphatically convey that at this present time, one out of every 3.7 females and 4.1 males will be sexually abused by the age of 22. The statistics regarding females has remained consistent over the last decade. Concerning males in our society, the degree of abuse has consistently gone up over the last decade.

Unfortunately, the degree of sexual abuse regarding children 6 years of age and under has increased significantly as well. Many attribute this to the increase in child pornography. When one considers the reality of these statistics, due to their overwhelming nature, they are difficult to believe.

These statistics translate into, in America, millions of individuals having experienced some form of sexual abuse. To put this into perspective, think of it this way: in a major university, such as Ohio State, where there are approximately 100,000 students, 25,000 of the students attending this university have or will experience some form of sexual abuse.

In a local High School, where 4,000 students attend, almost 1,000 students will have experienced some form of sexual abuse. To make it even more personal, if you live in a housing complex where there are 40 homes in your neighborhood, almost 10 of these homes would have someone in their household affected by some form of sexual abuse.

To be quite honest, I heard these statistics referenced over and over again in both my undergraduate and graduate studies, but never really believed them. They were so overwhelming that it was difficult to accept. It was an experience that took place while my wife and I were involved in campus ministry that changed this mindset.

A freshmen student came to us sharing of her being sexually abused. We worked with her regarding the healing process. While leading a Bible study, this same girl shared of her being harmed and then helped. There were 8 students in her study. Six of them shared that they had been sexually abused as well.

This caused us to own up to the prevalence of sexual abuse and to make it a priority in counseling. Sexual abuse involves those of all races, incomes, educational backgrounds, and environments. It affects equally those from urban, suburban, and rural areas.

Also, the perpetrators come from every stratum of society. This includes family members, peers, helpers, authority figures, and more random people.

Family

It is hard to understand but uncles, aunts, grandfathers, siblings (both step & natural), and cousins are among those causing harm. As well, live-in boyfriends are a significant source of abuse.

Peers

Unfortunately, numerous children have been hurt by other children. For example, a seven-year-old has been sexually abused by a baby sitter. Then the 7-year-old does the same to his four-year-old neighbor.

In this context, I think of a young boy who was abused by an adult while his parents were doing drugs downstairs. Unfortunately, he hurt numerous children his age before he was found out. I do not share this to bring fear as there is provision regarding such situations, which will be shared. As well, over half of dates rapes are caused by someone the victim knew well.

Helpers

Helpers include babysitters, tutors, and aides. It involves anyone who is entrusted to help your child in a specific way. Unfortunately, a significant number of those entrusted with children are not trustworthy. Regarding babysitting, this is an area of special concern.

Authority Figures – Role Models

This includes teachers, coaches, doctors, dance instructors, youth group leaders, policemen, scout leaders, and political figures. This is a situation where the position and age of the authority figures and supposed role models create an imbalanced relationship. This category of abuse is especially difficult to discuss due to the extreme vulnerability of the victim.

Recently, a doctor working with female gymnasts, several of whom became Olympic medalists was convicted for sexually abusing hundreds of these precious girls. These horrendous acts took place over decades. Some of these precious young women were asked why they were not more assertive when being harmed. They shared that they tried to tell significant others, but were not able and when they did, nothing was done.

Most do not realize the power, the intrinsic dominance that an authority figure has regarding those he or she is supposed to teach and protect. Just a few years ago, we had to expand our center due to the number of younger children who have been harmed.

However, it is not only small children. It includes all scenarios where the variable of imbalanced relationships exists. Years ago, my former student teaching advisor, shared this with me. He was teaching a very competitive graduate course.

The first day of the class, after introductions, he instructed them to do the following. He told them to take out a piece of paper, crumple it up and then chew it. To his surprise, a number of individuals in the class did just that. I would never have thought that anyone would, but they did. How much more do you think a child is susceptible to the wrong doing of a tutor, a teacher, a minister, or a coach?

Truly, most in a position of authority are very trustworthy. However, many are not. From movie directors to police officers and military personnel to politicians, to clergy, one needs to error on the side of caution.

Again, this is not to bring fear, but to simply convey the reality of today's society. However, there truly is provision.

Military Scenario

The pentagon in a well-publicized report stated that in 2013 that up to 20,000 military members experienced some sort of sexual assault.

The number alone speaks for itself. I have counseled so many that upon entrance to serving their country never expected to have to deal with sexual harassment and even assault.

This is the reason that these areas of challenge are being presented. As parents, we need to be ready for the challenges that they will face regarding their safety.

As a side note, even though the degree of sexual harassment and assault is appalling, the definite majority of military personnel are not involved.

Opioid Addiction

The prevalence of opioid addiction is simply hard to comprehend. It transcends economics, race, geography, gender, and most age groups. Just recently, I have counseled various individuals who have been brought back from the brink of death by Narcan an average of 5 times. Many of these adolescents never thought that they would be in this situation. They are trying desperately to be free.

There are answers, our counseling deals with root issues in the context of cause and effect. Personal responsibility is also emphasized. Some keys are education, communication, and starting early. The opioid epidemic exemplifies so strongly what both children and parents are facing in today's society.

As well, those promoting drugs for their own gain are much more prescribed than most realize. Dealers go to youth in the malls handing out opioids for free. They do this knowing that approximately 15% of those who do Heroin one time will become instantly addicted. An older brother has his sibling give out opioids to fellow 6th graders knowing the outcome. Herein, we as parents and educators need to be equally intentional in what we do to combat it.

Bullying

Bullying is an issue in the past few years that has been much more visible to the public. The idea that sticks and stones can break my bones, but names can never hurt me is being seen as totally false. Our children are vulnerable to their peers, in that their identity is in the process of being formed.

In the process, they have difficulty seeing the end from immediate pressure that they are experiencing. When one or a multiple individuals target them to degrade an identity that is not yet formed, it seems like the whole world is against them. Very simply, no one is meant to be bullied. One needs to understand that in the development process, our children are extremely vulnerable.

I have counseled people who vividly remember experiences from decades prior when they were bullied. The pain is still there if they have not been healed. This is because at certain ages we are extremely vulnerable to other people's actions and words. Prior to this decade, bullying was accepted to a large degree as normal. Thankfully, it is now being seen as what it really is, filthy, abnormal, and destructive.

At the same time, it is still very prevalent. In fact, with Facebook, and other social medias; Cyber-Bullying, causes bullying to be even more pervasive. Herein, it is necessary to proactively address it.

Domestic Abuse

In today's society, one would not think that domestic abuse would be prevalent, but it is. Wives are still being abused by husbands, and at times, vice versa. Children unfortunately are being harmed as well. The key is zero tolerance. This includes immediate responses to negate harm and facilitate safety.

Negative Internet Influence

The internet to such a large degree is unregulated. It is a breeding place for perpetrators. Many of these predators are professional like in their ability to deceive. As well, it is a primary vehicle of peer interaction, with this interaction being unmonitored it is a place where many lives are harmed.

The internet is also a premier information source. This can be both beneficial or detrimental. It is detrimental in that individuals struggling with their identity are predisposed to being exploited. Websites promoting evil, how to make bombs, and vengeance abound.

Adolescents struggling to find their identity will do almost anything just for "likes". In fact, just recently numerous young people risked their lives by eating tide pods just to obtain "likes". It is imperative that the internet be monitored by you, as a parent.

Pornography

Pornography is more accessible than ever before, from the internet, to video games, and magazines, to books, and movies. Our counseling center deals with this issue regarding both men and women. The definite majority of individuals struggling with pornography were introduced to this medium between the ages of ten to fourteen.

The effects of pornography can last a lifetime, including sexual addiction. As with all of the ways in which our children can be harmed, it is difficult to hear. However, there is definite provision to overcome which will be conveyed in our ensuing chapter.

Video Games

In almost 40 years of counseling I have seen many children affected adversely due to video games. Most parents honestly do not know the content of most of the games that are on the market today. So many include a very high degree of violence, degradation of women, and sexually oriented material. The degree of violence is very disturbing.

What one needs to consider is why so many of our youth are angry. They are angry due to divorce, they are angry because they are being bullied, and due to feeling hopeless, due to outward failure. Some feel that it is good to engage in this type of gaming. They see it as a vehicle to sublimate their anger.

However, all too often it turns into a mindset of violence that is integrated into their own lives. Herein, it truly needs to be monitored.

Depression

Depression is more prevalent in our society regarding our children than ever before. From minimal depression to strong clinical depression, our children are having to deal with the issue.

In prior decades, depression was seen as something that was the fault of the individual who was suffering.

Accordingly, the person was just told to measure up and they would be okay.

Now, we know that it is a problem that is not the individual's fault. It is a sickness that nobody asked for. Herein, it is imperative that we understand what the signs of depression are and how to affirm our children.

In the context of this affirmation, an individual treatment plan can then be prescribed and carried out.

Suicide

Unfortunately, as depression in our children is significantly increasing, so is suicide. In fact, suicide is now the 10th leading cause of death in the United States.

It is hard to comprehend, but in our provision chapter we will share the reasons for this.

As well, we will share common sense solutions to this tragic reality. It used to be when this topic was discussed in a public forum, a handful of people would show up. Now, scores of people show up, this concern speaks for itself.

Vehicular Accidents

Vehicular safety is a primary concern of all parents. Recently, I did counseling in a school district where a number of students were killed in 3 different accidents.

In this context, I spent significant time with State Police officials. There are specific things that we can do in a very intentional fashion to help our children in this area. This area includes not only cars and trucks, but all vehicles.

Sports

Sports are a part of societies across the globe. They provide an outlet for our children that for many is an integral part of their growth process. Recently, much attention has been given to the prevalence of concussions related to football. It is something parents need to profoundly be aware of. Concussions are also prevalent in soccer through heading the ball and the game in general.

All sports need to be monitored closely and appropriate safety measures have to be put into place. Interestingly enough, one of the sports where the most injuries occur is in cheerleading.

Whether it is motocross, skiing, or skateboarding, most accidents are preventable. In this truth, parents can proactively protect their children in their sports participation.

Fads

Our children are very impressionable. Herein, fads can influence them through their peers or the internet. One surprising fad that is in vogue is the Tide pod challenge. It is where adolescents are seen on Facebook literally digesting Tide detergent pods to accumulate "likes". To the surprise and sadness of many, a number of teens have died due to this fad.

Fads like this seem far-fetched and many times are not taken seriously. Very simply, they need to be. Other current and sustained fads include the choking game, 50 shades of gray parties, super shots, and glue bags.

Abduction

As never before, children are at risk regarding abduction. Whether it is due to the increase in mental illness, child pornography addiction, or trafficking, the risk is real. One needs to error on the side of caution regarding their children. As with all of the areas of risk, it is an inconvenient truth. Whether at Walmart, a sporting event, or taking young children to the park, learning how to be environmentally aware is a key.

Violence

Violence is a reality in culture. It is intrinsic to our movies, television, sports, and gaming. Consequently, it translates into violent encounters in our schools, general peer interaction, and in organizations that promote hazing. Again, it is imperative that we equip our children with wisdom and use commonsense to direct their steps.

This includes knowing geographically what an area entails in this context. Violence is now integrated into our culture in a very strong way. However, this does not mean it has to be integrated into your family.

Sickness

Sickness is something that obviously can bring harm to our children. Very simply, it is important to error on the side of caution when our children are sick. We need to utilize medical help as needed. As well, we need to be proactive in the context of prevention. We need to keep our children away from harmful diets, second-hand smoke, and things like mold.

As well, we need to address areas of concern. I was working with administrators in a catholic high school recently. It was in a very prestigious area. One of the head administrators came to me after our meeting and asked me the following. He asked "So many of our students are struggling with Asthma. Do you know why this might be?" I shared my opinion with him, but I share with you that in instances like this, it is good to investigate.

Accidents

Due to small children obtaining medicine in a cabinet, to pools not fenced in, to unlocked gun cabinets accidents do occur. Provision will be given regarding these and other areas regarding accidents.

School Shootings

Much attention has recently been given to school safety and rightly so. I served for years as a member of the safety committee as a school board member. Most do not realize the degree of intentionality intrinsic to most shootings. This is difficult to understand. However, due to the degree of intentionality, proactive measures, when put in place, can bring a high degree of safety in our schools.

I know that the 14 areas of potential harm can seem overwhelming. However, in the context of wisdom, they had to be shared. This is because in order to defeat the enemies of safety, we need to know what they are.

The exciting thing is that regarding every area of harm, there are provisions that will procure safety for your children and give you a confidence that you have never had before.

Chapter 3

Parental Attributes

The foundation of child safety is parental character. As with anything, success is determined by the ability of an individual or individuals to implement a prescribed plan. The plan regarding provision will be conveyed in the ensuing chapters. That which constitutes parental proficiency will be emphasized now.

As we focus on the primary traits necessary for parental proficiency, I want to preface our sharing with the following. No parent is going to be perfect. What we are focusing on isn't conveying expectations that are unrealistic. We are focusing on an attitude of commitment that is necessary for your child's safety. It is a commitment that every parent is capable of fulfilling.

You're reading this text in your endeavoring to be the best parent you can is certainly a strong positive in itself.

Assertiveness and Courage

Regarding safety and primary parental attributes, we will focus on four main traits. The first area revolves around assertiveness and courage. Most people do not enjoy confrontation, even when it involves family. Herein, many times it is easier to avoid confrontation even when we need to be assertive.

This is especially true when our personalities gravitate toward being quiet or being non-confrontational. Due to the significance of this trait. I am going to share 3 experiences, one of which is personal in order to help us see what this trait entails.

Underage Drinking Party at Home

While teaching high school years ago, I became aware as many did of many athletes attending an underage drinking party at one of the student's houses in a nearby town. The parents of this student rationalized the parties this way. The students are going to drink no matter what we do. Consequently, we will provide the alcohol and let them drink in the confines of our home.

I counseled parents of an 11th grader who attended the parties. They knew that it was not right but let him go. They did this due to the parents' (who held the party) seemly position in the community.

Unfortunately, their son was a passenger in a car driven by another student that wrecked. He survived but was injured. His parents came to me guilt ridden. Their lack of assertiveness and courage almost cost them their son.

One definition of assertiveness is doing what you know is the right thing to do. Intrinsic to this definition is courage. This is because it is not always easy to do. You are not to be condemned for struggling in this area. However, it is necessary that we do what we need to do for the sake of our children.

A Bad Reputation

The next example is similar to the first in that it involves significant decision making. Pertinent information such as names have been changed to assure anonymity. "Sally" is a sophomore who obtained a medium part in the high school play. Her friend "Tom" is a nice young man but has a bad reputation due to driving too fast. Sally's parents know this and accordingly would not allow her to be a passenger in his car.

However, Tom and some of her friends gave Sally a hard time. They said that she simply thought that she was better than them. Sally struggled with her self-concept and her parents were influenced by this. Seeing her down, they succumbed to letting her ride with Tom.

However, on a late February snowy day, Tom was driving too fast for road conditions. The car skidded and went into an embankment.

Injuries in this case were limited. However, it does not always turn out this well. The amazing thing in this scenario was that Tom and his friends downplayed the incident and still accused Sally of being the problem. This shows that you are never going to please everyone.

<u>My Story</u>

Regarding this trait, it is sometimes easier said than done. Years ago, there was ice on the road and I asked my daughter not to go out, knowing it was unsafe. My daughter disagreed and felt that I was over stepping my bounds. I came real close to letting her drive with her friend, but I did not. It was not a popular decision. However, that night, there were different accidents. She later shared that she appreciated my concern for her.

All of us to some degree struggle in this area. This is due to a number of reasons. They include general insecurity, fear of rejection, being hurt when involved in standing up for right, different types of personalities, and inferiority.

The key to entering into being assertive and courageous is 4-fold. First and foremost, it is all about motivation. You may struggle with insecurity but to keep your children secure, you have to be more concerned about their safety than your struggle with insecurity.

Second, is to know how important it is to live according to your heart as a parent. Within every parent is an innate heart need to protect their child. We need to know that as we act with our heart, even when we feel weak that our heart will take over. Parenting from the heart is powerful. It is what our children need. It conveys to them that in our hearts, they are our first priority.

Third, we are all under construction. We are all in need of help to strengthen us. Whether, it is through our faith or the help of positive role models, we need to grow in this area for the sake of our children.

Lastly, I find that simulating possible circumstances that could arise with your children is of great benefit. This can be done through simply talking about different situations and how you would respond.

Role play can also be incorporated into this simulation. For example, the following scenarios could be a point of focus.

* What would we do if a close relative or good friend invited our child over for a sleepover with an older son in the house who struggles with pornography?

* What would we do if a child in our child's fifth grade class was bullying a friend of his through physical threats, but that the principal said that it was unfounded?

*What would we do if our child who is a very good baseball player said he did not want to go out for the 9th grade team because of a hazing ritual that upper classmen would make him go through?

*What would you do if a very popular coach seemed to look at your 8th grade daughter in an inappropriate way?

*What would we do if after telling our 18-year-old that he or she could not go with their 2 friends waiting outside in a car to a party that we know is bad and they start walking out the door anyway?

*What would you do if you simply didn't feel at peace with your 6-year-old child being babysat by your aunt who is trustworthy and her new husband (you just sense something is not right with him)?

You can put in many other scenarios that are applicable to you. Wisdom is dealing with situations preemptively. It is being ready for situations that we may face. It is not first dealing with the situation after the fact. It is proactively being ahead of the curve.

Communication

Our second parental attribute is the commitment to be communicative regarding our children. Strong communication with our children is not an option, it is a necessity. This is due to communication being the vehicle that relationship is built upon. It is powerful in that it cultivates relationship in 7 ways.

Expression of Love

Communication expresses the love within our heart regarding those who are most significant to us. Many parents love their children but do not express that love fully. Due to up-bringing, personality or simply not taking time, the love within their heart is concealed rather than expressed.

It is vital to communicate with our children because they so much need the love within their parents to be expressed to them. This expression of love needs to be communicated from birth and continue in all stages unto adulthood.

It is amazing how much a young child can interact and be communicated with. A toddler can understand both love and rejection. As he or she grows, heart to heart communication is the key.

Degree of Commitment

Communication is truly indicative of your commitment to your child. Communication involves time and the sharing of your heart with your child. When you make your children a priority in the context of time and energy, it tells your child that they are valuable. It tells them that you are truly committed to them.

<u>Impartation</u>

The third way that communication brings forth relationship is through impartation. As a parent, you have a desire for what you know to be good to be given to your children. This includes morality, attitude, thankfulness, work ethic, convictions, and interests. This is why you see babies with Pittsburgh Steeler booties or Nascar caps on them! You want to share with your child what is important to you.

It is so significant that you talk to your children. From an early age, you want to teach them about life. You want to give them an understanding of why things are and how they can impact others. This will translate into them not just knowing the facts but having a love of learning. You can teach them how to problem solve effectively from a young age.

Statistics show that when families that play different types of board games together from an early age that academic achievement goes up and closer relationships result. This is such a simple example, but it shows you the power of interaction. As parents, you have such an awesome opportunity to influence your child unto greatness!

Child rearing is not just a responsibility. It is an amazing adventure that can realize strength in your children that only you can give. Herein, I want to encourage you to do this simple exercise.

Write down the vision, the primary desires that you want to see fulfilled regarding your child. Then write down seven ways that you believe will bring these desires into realization. Then, each month check to see if these different ways are being implemented as you intend.

This simple paradigm does 3 things. First, it gives intentionality to your parenting. Second, it shows you that you are the key to these desires being realized. Lastly, it brings a degree of accountability to your parenting.

Example Chart

Traits in your Child	Process
1. Moral, Loving	1. Communication through encouragement, family time, and discussion
2. Independent Thinking – Problem Solving	2. Love for reading, problem solving together
3. Confident	3. Participation in athletics, dance, and debate team
4. Thankful	4. Church involvement, utilize real life situations. Visit homeless shelters
5. Entrepreneurial	5. Learning ways to earn money

6. Compassion	6. Monthly visits to homeless shelters and/or convalescent homes
7. Courage	7. Reading stories of those who were courageous

Recently, I shared this paradigm with a couple and then asked them what their vision was for their children. They were an African American couple who had 3 young boys. They immediately responded by saying "we are raising our boys to be amazing husbands who glorify God." Wow! It was not a coincidence that these young boys, ages 7,9, & 11were some of the most respectful, bright, and moral young men that I have ever met.

What would our society be like if we followed these parents in their pursuit? From experience I know that a number of parents do not feel confident regarding this area of communication. This can be due to up-bringing, not feeling "professional" enough or from simply feeling overwhelmed with life in general.

Consequently, we let the teacher, the coach, the youth pastor, and the television be preeminent regarding our children. None of the above are wrong, they can all be beneficial. However, they cannot replace you. You might not know as much as the teacher, however, when problem solving with your child, it does more than any teacher can.

You might not know as much as the baseball coach, but when you play catch with your child, it supersedes anything a coach can ever do. You might not know the Bible quite as well as a pastor, but when you pray with your child, it influences him or her more than any pastor ever could. The television can show a sitcom or a movie. However, it cannot in anyway compare to their spending time with you. This is because parental communication comes from the heart. It is a heart filled with a love that only the heart of a parent contains.

<u>Intimacy</u>

In the heart of every child is a profound need to be loved by his parents. This is innate, this is why it is so important to communicate encouragement and true identity to your child.

Words of negativity and degradation pierce deeply. Phrases like, "he will never succeed, she can never do anything right, he just doesn't have it like his brother," can produce according to the seed that is sown.

However, if negative words and attitudes can produce harm, how much more can words of esteem, encouragement, and edification produce strength and enlightenment regarding their true identity? The hearts of our children are soft and impressionable.

They are in need of words and attitudes of affirmation. A parent rejoices when their child excels. A parent hurts when their child fails. A parent believes in them when they are doing wrong.

A parent will give all when their child needs it. A parent speaks true identity to their child unto his or her identity being formed.

I will never forget an experience I had many years ago. My wife and I asked an older woman to babysit our daughter. When we came back, she was rocking her in a chair. In the space of about two minutes, I heard her tell our young child "you are awesome, you are so smart, you are amazing!" I thought to myself, no wonder her son is the presiding judge in our county!

We need to communicate the awesomeness of who our children are unto them truly knowing it. As well, not only with words but with emotions, we need to communicate.

When your child is hurting, it is good at times to cry with them. In times when they hurt you in their growth process, it is good for them to see your tears of hurt. Love that is concealed can never bear fruit. Love that is revealed, communicated will bear the fruit of intimacy for a life time.

Life

Life is truly good, but there are times of challenge. In both good and tough times, it is critical to communicate. Herein, you need to develop a pattern of transparency wherein open communication is the norm.

Never assume all is well. Through spending quality time consistently, regardless of age, let your children see your heart. Let them see how significant they are to you, how you need their interaction.

They need to see that you need to know how they are doing, in both accomplishment and struggle. They need to know that they are a part of your life that you will never be able to do without. Life is all about relationship. Relationship is all about communication.

Knowing Your Child

Every child is certainly unique. However, in our humanness, it is easy to fall prey to the natural guise of assumption. If we have one child, we assume that they are like us. I we have multiple children, we assume they are all very similar.

In reality, children are indeed different. It is imperative that we understand these differences and interact accordingly. This is why this third trait of knowing your child is so important.

Many are familiar with the book *The Five Love Languages*, authored by Dr. Gary Chapman. There is tremendous wisdom intrinsic to this text. It is an invaluable tool regarding the marriage relationship.

The 5 Love Languages include verbal affirmation, time, gifts, touch, and acts of service. If one spouse primarily desires love to be expressed in verbal affirmation and the other expresses love through acts of service, there can be a problem!

Herein, it is beneficial to know your spouse's perception of how love is to be conveyed. In general, it is wisdom to know how an individual perceives things. Incidentally, there is a *5 Love Languages* book for children as well. The key is knowing the strength and weaknesses of your children and how they react to different situations.

My first daughter learned to drive very quickly she was on the main road in a few days with no problems. Accordingly, I expected my second daughter to learn likewise.

However, as she drove over the curb and into someone's yard, I thought differently and changed course. Both are good drivers today but got there in different ways. Had I not changed plans, it would have been a very frustrating time for both of us!

There are 7 main areas regarding our children that we need to be able to discern. They include personality, predispositions to harm, reactions to failure or pain, giftings and talents, learning modalities, peer interaction, and love languages.

Personality

There are numerous personality tests on the market today. They are easy to take and interpret. Most categorize individuals within 4 basic personality makeups. They include outgoing, dominant, quiet, or service oriented.

Sometimes children will have a personality consistent with both parents. Sometimes their personality will gravitate more towards one parent than another. It is so important that we do not esteem one personality above another.

Different times, a parent will put one child above another due to their personality being more like theirs. This is incredibly wrong and can be very detrimental to all involved.

A child who is more outgoing is usually more emotional than the others. This can be good and bad. They are usually more sensitive and can get their feelings hurt in a strong way. However, they can be the life of the party, they have an ability to attract people to them and like to stand out. Consequently, as a parent you have to reel in emotions whether too high or too low. Relationally and in general expectation of others are very high and need to be balanced out.

Intrinsic to the dominant personality is usually being independent and having a desire to lead others. Even at a young age, children with this personality can be misperceived as rebellious and not nice.

This is due to them being more independent. A while ago, I counseled a mom who was very distraught. She had two boys, ages 7 and 10 who were giving her real attitude problems.

They were good kids but needed to be seen in a certain way. Certainly, they needed to be disciplined at times. However, they were not bad or rebellious. They simply had a very dominant personality.

I told them that they would be very successful in life. They were a challenge at times but they are doing exceptionally well at this time.

Predisposition to Harm

All our children will encounter potential harm in the context of their makeup. Harm comes in two main ways. They are reactions to temptations and reactions to hurt or perceived hurt.

Temptations

Temptations include drugs, sexual immorality, crime, excessive risk taking, and inappropriate peer relationships. The key to understanding the degree of vulnerability that your child has towards these temptations is the word predispositional.

Predisposition means that you are susceptible to something. There is something in you that makes you susceptible. That something in a child does not mean that they are bad or will succumb to temptation. However, it does mean that parents need to be aware of the predisposition because it needs to be addressed.

As a parent, you become aware by seeing the necessity to be aware and then taking time to do so. This is the key. Herein, you make a simple evaluation regarding predispositions to different things. As you observe your child, ask yourself 4 things. Is he or she overly influenced by their peers? Is he or she one who thinks before they act or are they primarily reactive? Does your child act favorable to correction? Does he or she outwardly struggle when not accepted?

Awareness comes through your observation, but it also comes from the observations of others. This may include a sibling, teacher, or youth pastor. Lastly, it is good to bring up situations and ask questions regarding possible struggles.

According to what you see, you then address. You can teach on assertiveness and saying no. You can teach on how to control emotions and not being reactive. As well, you can reinforce the strengthens within your child and teach how to utilize them more effectively.

Reactions to Hurt or Perceived Hurt

Hurt can take many forms. From abuse and bullying, to unfilled expectations, it can have a very detrimental effect. Even as hurt can take many forms, so is the effect that it has on our children.

Again, every child is different, the key is understanding the differences. As with our prior area, we ask the same questions and utilize observation as well to evaluate.

However, regarding reaction to hurt or perceived hurt, the variable of sensitivity is different in each child as well. Sensitivity entails the degree that one's emotions are affected by difficult situations. Sensitivity is certainly not bad in itself. In fact, it is a gift in the sense that one can identify with the hurts of others and be compassionate and merciful.

However, it can also be a negative in regard to reactions. This is due to being more apt to internalize the pain. The internalization accentuates both the pain and an inability to get over it. Again, every child is different. However, most invariably, when one is harmed four phases of coping take place. These phases include in order denial, anger, depression, and an effort to do what is necessary to overcome.

Let's look at a simple example. Jimmy is a good football player who has practiced all season for his senior year. Unfortunately, just prior to his first game, he goes down with a season ending injury. Jimmy's reaction is normal. He is first in denial. He knows that he will not play the rest of the season but does not accept this. Usually the denial turns into anger. Why me? All the work that I did has been for nothing. It is just not fair.

Then anger usually phases into mild depression. You feel bad, you feel sorry for yourself. You don't feel like engaging in activities as you normally would. Lastly, depression phases into seeing things more clearly. You start to see the composite, the big picture. Accordingly, you modify your plans and begin to deal with things the best that you can.

Things become dangerous for a child when they get stuck in a phase or that phase is overly accentuated. For example, when denial is realized through drug use.

I am reminded of a young man who was an exceptional athlete whose season did end with injury. He turned to drugs to escape the reality of the disappointment. It took him a long time to recover. Some who have been bullied, abused or disappointed have never gotten over the anger phase. They become hurtful and even vindictive. This is when road rage and gun violence can take place.

There are others who stay in the depression phase. They simply lose hope regarding blessing and success. They cannot see light at the end of the tunnel even though many times they are very able to succeed.

In the last phase, one will start to deal with the situation and get on with their life. Unfortunately, some will deal with it through perfectionism. They do this thinking that if they do everything right at this time, it will stave off future harm. This of course is not true. You can tell a lot about your child regarding how they react regarding these phases. If they are overreacting or stuck in a phase, this is an opportunity to help them through it.

However, if you are not being observant, you will not be able to help them as they need you to. Recently, I had parents come into the office due to their child not doing well in school. He was twelve years old. He shared with me openly about not being accepted by his peers. As well, he shared that he was doing video games 5 to 7 hours a day.

His parents both worked 2 jobs and were unaware of both of these things. He was crying out for help and they really didn't see it.

Thankfully, appropriate intervention took place, but it doesn't always happen. Your child from a young age responds differently to things. Accordingly, it is a key to know how to respond to him or her.

Strength and Weakness

Every child has strengths and weaknesses. It is imperative that we know them. Success brings more and more success. As well, failure breeds failure. All too often, children are put into molds that are inconsistent with who they really are. These molds can be who we think they should be as opposed to who they are.

I coached cross-country and track in high school. One of my best runners won a district champions her junior year. Prior to this, she played basketball. She was horrible at basketball! However, her dad loved basketball. She played due to his love for basketball but hated it. Finally, he agreed to encourage her to run. He was glad he did because it released her gifting and she obtained a scholarship to run in college.

A while ago, I was working with 2 college students who both had been accepted to medical school. One was the son of a doctor and to be honest, he struggled in school regarding the sciences. The other was gifted in the sciences.

In the first year of medical school, the doctor's son called me. He was miserable and only in medical school to please his parents. I encouraged him to not be pressured but to pursue his destiny according to his God given abilities. His parents understood. He actually obtained a doctorate in a mental health field and is doing great today.

Parents need to work with their children regarding both their weaknesses and strengths. Weaknesses need to be worked on through specific strategies, patience, and encouragement.

Strengths need to be accentuated and cultivated. Even where there are strengths. There will be challenges. Herein, encouragement and patience are necessary regarding strengths as well.

The key to knowing your child is understanding that knowing your child is a parental key. The more that you know your child, the more you will be able to meet their needs. As well, you will be able to bring them into a paradigm of success that promotes confidence and self-esteem.

Role Model

Our fourth main parental trait is that of being a role model. Intrinsic to a child is a desire to be like mom and dad. The influence that parents have on their children is exponential.

Consequently, the life that you live is profoundly significant. It is one thing to tell your children what they should do and how they should live. However, your admonitions and instructions have to be reinforced by the life that you live.

When your life is commensurate with what you say and desire in your children, it gives great strength to your children. Now, being an appropriate role model does not mean that you do everything perfectly. It simply means that you are sincerely doing the best that you can.

The identity of our children is that which is established over time. It is very progressive. Herein, as parents, we need to be consistent in our lifestyle.

To be quite honest, the most difficult counseling situations that I have encountered in the last 35 years involve this variable of parental lifestyle. One young man who was referred to our counseling center was extremely angry. This anger translated into fighting, drug abuse, and several suspensions from school.

Through counseling I came to learn that his parents were very reputable in the community and were very involved in church. I also came to learn that his dad had physically struck him on several occasions. It is one thing to be hit on the playground in a fight. It is entirely another thing to be hit by the hand of the one that is supposed to be your primary role model.

I integrated the parents into the counseling process. The father readily admitted to hurting his son. However, he started to make excuses and tried to minimize the effects of his actions.

Consequently, I asked to meet with him privately. In a controlled but assertive fashion I shared with him the consequents of his actions. In this reality, he put his head down and stopped making excuses. Over time, with a great change in his attitude, relationship with his son was restored. Unfortunately, it does not always turn out this way. In our society today, many parents are all about themselves. I come to the game if my child is starting. We affirm success but struggle to walk through the times of difficultly with our children.

As a parent, you may be struggling with issues in your own life. You may be incredibly stressed with trying to make ends meet. However, it is imperative that we see that raising our children is the greatest privilege of life. Their world revolves around you. From birth, the only world that they know is the world that you present to them. The only life that they perceive is the life that you live before them. It is an awesome responsibility. However, inside every parent is an innate desire to fulfill this responsibility.

Conclusion

The four parental attributes that we have discussed are truly the foundation of parenting. They translate into both joy and protection for your children. At the same time, they are attributes that require commitment. They require commitment in the context of both time and in regard to personal growth. We are all so busy. It certainly is easier not to deal with issues. It is certainly easier not take time to communicate fully.

However, how one's time is prioritized is the true gauge of relationship. True relationship involves truly focusing on the ones that you love. It comes down to loving our children sacrificially. It comes down to being so motivated due to who they are to us, that we do what they need us to be.

The commitment to cultivate these four traits is challenging as well. They simply do not magically appear! They are cultivated through focus, continued learning via books and seminars, and spousal interaction. As well, interacting with other parents who have the same parental passion is always a key.

An athlete doesn't become an all-star overnight. A student does not obtain a degree in one semester. You, as a parent grow daily. You are the key to your child growing and developing. It is the greatest joy of life to grow and develop together.

Chapter 4

Twenty-nine Wisdom Keys of Prevention

The following wisdom keys are life changing. Just one of these keys discovered can change your life as a parent and the life of your child. Wisdom is the key to success. It causes us to obtain knowledge and then enables us to utilize the knowledge obtained.

In regards to keeping our children safe, it is imperative that we are proactive. The specific wisdom keys of prevention will cause you to confidently be ahead of the curve. They will enable you to equip and stand up for your children. They will enable you to be able to enjoy your children without fear.

Our first five keys revolve around the parent-child relationship. This may not seem like it addresses specific safety concerns, but it is really the key. This is because when there is a close relationship with your child, this is when they will listen to you regarding what can harm them. This is also that which will cause them to share with you what they are really feeling, what they are really going through,

#1 Communicate from an Early Age

It is amazing how a young child can assimilate truth. It of course has to be presented in an age appropriate fashion they truly can receive much. The first five years of age are profoundly significant. This is the time to establish strong communication.

#2 Words of Affirmation

Affirm them with words of encouragement. Tell them of how awesome they are. Affirm they with joy and excitement. When they do something wrong, tell them that they will do better next time. Let them know that they can and will do amazing things. Accentuate both their giftings and accomplishments.

#3 Words of Love

Tell them how much they mean to you. Tell them how much you love them. This includes both parents. Again, start at an early age and let it continue unto adulthood and beyond! One parent may not feel as confident in expressing his or her love verbally or with a hug. Do it anyways! It is in you! Express it, your child needs you to do this and your heart needs to do it as well.

#4 Interact

You can interact through age appropriate games and learning activities. You can interact through watching a movie or playing catch. The key is showing that you want to be with them in a great way.

#5 Love for Learning

Instill in them not only knowledge but a love for learning. Ask them questions, learn together. Through books, a camping trip or a visit to the museum, learn and explore together. Again, start at an early age and let it continue unto adulthood and beyond!

#6 *Investigation and Information*

Do not make a decision involving your child without having knowledge to back your decision. If you are choosing a daycare center, simply do not take things at face value. Talk to the director. **Ask Questions!**

*There is a question sheet regarding daycare that will assist you in the back of this text.

In assisting a single mom recently, my wife and I were unpleasantly surprised at the true environment that was present at a certain daycare place.

One director had her boyfriend helping her who had just gotten out of prison. Another did not do background checks. Another center that is well known nationally did not deal with children who were biting other children, having no written due process.

You cannot assume. You have to have information that enables you to make an informed decision.

I cannot underestimate the significance of background checks. As well, ask those that you trust about the coach your child will play for and the guitar instructor that will interact with your child. The information can be extremely beneficial.

Babysitting Forms

Unfortunately, a high percentage of incurred sexual abuse comes at the hands of babysitters. This does not discount the trustworthiness of most, but it is an area which is truly problematic.

*Herein, a babysitter application is included in the back of the text. You can look at it right now.

I am amazed how we as parents who truly love our children do not act with more diligence in this area. Years ago, I knew that even with our children, my wife and I should have been more careful. Different times we called a friend of a person we knew.

However, we really did not know them nor did we take time to know them. Thankfully, no harm was done, but it could easily have. You simply cannot assume that everyone is trustworthy.

You check out a car before you buy it. You check out a house before you would live in it. How much more should we get to know the person that we literally entrust our children to? You would be surprised how the simple babysitting application referred to weeds out many who were high risk. Again, we need to obtain the information we need.

Regarding babysitting, simply ask yourself, can I fully trust all those who will be present? This includes the primary sitter and those who have the potential to be present. If you know that Uncle George or Cousin Bob are unstable in anyway and may be present, do not put your children in harm's way.

You are not being obsessive, you are being a good parent protecting your child.

Again, simply ask yourself this question. Am I confident, do I know for sure that I can trust that there will not be the potential for harm in any way to my children through their presence?

The same principle applies to sleepovers. Most sleepovers, whether with just one friend spending the night or a group of girls getting together promote harmony and not harm. However, if variables of safety are not in place, sleepovers can become a nightmare that can last a lifetime. This is the truth.

A nine-year-old-boy ends up being harmed by an older brother of the friend he is sleeping over with. A 14-year-old-girl is wrongly touched by the step dad of her close friend. A sleepover for junior high girls is not chaperoned as expected. Boys are invited, and sex games are initiated by a few of the boys and your child is truly hurt. It was not the desire of the child to enter into these games. It was the last thing that they desired to do. However, they were caught off guard. They went expecting a pajama party and were not prepared for what took place.

As with most of the scenarios like these, I have counseled those who have been hurt. I actually weep as I share this with you. However, there is provision. As with daycare and babysitting, a checklist is provided for you to help in making sure the sleepover environment will be safe.

You may say, why do I have to have a prescribed checklist? It is because many times persons of harm have their checklist. They are intentional and know when children are vulnerable. They are very prescribed.

*Some of the variables on the checklist include the following, many of these apply to children or any age:

*Will the sleepover be supervised sufficiently?

*Who will be those who will supervise?

*Will there be other individuals present that I am not aware of?

*What kind of games or movies will be played and viewed?

*Do any participants or their parents have a bad reputation?

*If older children, will those attending be leaving the house to drive to another location?

*What vehicle will be used and how many occupants will be in the vehicle?

*If camping out or playing in the woods nearby, is it a location where tics are prevalent?

*Is the house itself safe?

*If there is a pool involved, is it made inaccessible when there is no supervision?

*Will all firearms be out of reach of the children?

These are simple commonsensical variables. However, they are the cornerstone of safety. Unfortunately, they are all too often negated.

I shared this checklist with a high school guidance counselor recently. He wept as I shared them. A friend of the family's son was riding in the bed of a pick-up with four other boys joy riding. He fell out and was significantly injured. He looked at me and shared that he wished he had this checklist to give to parents prior to this incident.

#8 School Safety

Due to recent school shootings, school safety is now a focal point for the nation.

Regarding the safety of your child, you need to know the degree of safety that your school ensures your child. As a school board member of my local district, I served on the safety committee. I made sure that in regard to our budget, safety was a priority.

Years ago, I proposed the following and do so even more adamantly today. Every building in the school district should have the highest safety standards. This includes:

*Metal detectors at each primary entrance monitored by armed security guards for all who enter

*All doors locked at all times during school

*Entrance only given via intercom system of those validated by administration

*Will have to go through metal detectors monitored by security

*List of all individuals on file who are not allowed entrance in front of administrator at all times

*those allowed to pick up students must be authorized by parents and administration and must show photo ID

However, this should only be the beginning of school security. It should also include the following.

*Mandatory safety orientation for all school bus drivers i.e. how to identify bullying on the bus

*Cameras on all buses

*Monitors on buses as deemed necessary

So much of the bullying that exists takes place on buses. It is especially prevalent when a student is on the bus for over 20 minutes.

*Hall monitors

*Cafeteria monitors

*Restroom monitors

Monitors include aides, teachers, administrators, and professional security. This may seem excessive, but it is not. It will sharply negate bullying, drug use, fights, sexual assault, and gang collusions if applicable.

Equally important, it promotes an environment of safety. All monitors should be cautious, respectful, and positively engaging.

*All extracurricular activities should be realized under the safety guidelines that operate during the regular school day. All too often, this is not the case.

*The appropriate number of chaperones should always be in place before an activity can be approved.

On a personal note, as a student and as a teacher at chaperoned dances, I saw more bullying, fights, sexual assault, and drug use than one would think. As well, as a restroom monitor at the high school level, drug deals and use were certainly prevalent in this area.

Sometimes, we simply make things more complicated than they are. We simply need to be where problems can occur. Do you remember when you were in school? Simply ask your children who is dealing, who is bullying.

Ask if they know of any teacher who looks at students in a sexually suggestive manner, even though they are not involved. They usually can tell you. If they know, don't you think administrators should know?

When I was involved in the public-school system, I was involved with discipline. Some of my best references, when something bad happened were the custodians. They knew what was going on more than anyone. To ensure a safe school, everyone is to be part of the team that creates a safe environment.

I know that this is strong but it needs to be shared. We cannot afford to provide a sanctuary for anyone who would bring harm to our children. The school environment should be a sanctuary for academic and social growth. Every child deserves this.

Locker Checks

When I taught, we had local authorities do locker checks regarding drugs. It was a true deterrent. I believe it is equally necessary today.

School Policy

Policies can include the number of passengers a student driver can have. Statistically, the chances of an accident go up 100 percent when a student driver has 3 passengers as opposed to one.

School policies should be spelled out. There should be zero tolerance for racism, bullying, drugs, and sexual harassment.

If you as a parent do not see an area of concern covered by specific school policy, you need to be encouraged to share your input.

<u>Assemblies</u>

All schools should have assemblies dealing with the topics of bullying, drug abuse, sexual assault, and school safety. It is an opportunity that needs to be taken advantage of. It is to spell out ramifications for bullying, racism, and hate crimes. These policies then have to be enforced.

<u>Mental Health</u>

There has to be a team approach to this critical issue. Parents, siblings, peers, teachers, case workers, guidance counselors, and administrators need to work together. In today's society, there is an increased degree of depression, violent gaming, bullying, sexual abuse, and domestic abuse.

When you put these variables together, they spell trouble. Identification, intervention, and monitoring are essential. When red flags go up via Facebook, a conversation or observed change in personality, someone has to share the information with someone in authority.

Just recently, a school district about an hour away from me where one of my best friends teaches 5th grade, tragedy was adverted. A student heard another student talking about carrying out a shooting. She told her parents and the police were notified. When they went to his house, numerous weapons with a detailed plan were found. Truly, we need each other regarding school safety.

I have shared of the different aspects of school safety for one purpose. It is so that you as a parent can effectively evaluate and influence your school system.

You need to rate the schools that you are considering sending you children to. As well, you need to consider the temperament of your own child in this consideration. If your child is in a school system at this time, you need to do the same.

Just a few days ago, I was talking to a very precious young lady who was a junior in a city school. She came to my office with a friend and was crying almost uncontrollably. She stated that she was a failure because she was not able to continue in the school setting that she was in. She stated that she couldn't take any more of the bullying, the violence, and adverse peer pressure.

She felt like a failure for these reasons. First, if she would graduate from this school with a certain GPA (2.5), she would be given a significant scholarship towards the college or university of her choice.

Second, her parents, especially her dad would see her struggles and need of a new school environment as indicative of her just being soft and not trying hard enough.

Third, her best friend who was with her was making it. Why couldn't she? The bottom line was that this girl wasn't soft, and she was trying. In fact, a friend of hers had been shot at a nearby school. This girl simply needs a change of venue. She needs to be understood and encouraged. Thankfully, her friend was very supportive of her.

School safety is of critical importance. You would not buy a car that had a gas pedal that stuck or an engine that was smoking. Why would you be called excessive and or obsessive when you genuinely evaluate your school and make decisions based on that evaluation?

One other note, know what your children are being taught and the books that are being used. For example, there are companies producing history books that no longer hardly cover World War I, World War II, the Korean War or the Vietnam War.

They do this under the guise of war being bad and America being a nation of exclusivism. I think that most would disagree with this mindset, yet many parents never even look at the books that their children use.

Again, the school system is a key to our children's development. As parents, we need to make sure that it is serving our children with an environment of both safety and encouragement.

Higher Education

It is amazing to me how too many well-meaning parents disassociate themselves from their higher education students. It is almost like they no longer have a right to be involved in their lives now as they are entering into a new phase of life.

To be quite honest if you are helping pay for their education, you have a right. As well, if they are still bringing their laundry home, you have a right.

Mostly importantly, they need your support, wisdom, and interaction now more than ever before. This is because they will face challenges that they have never faced before. This is especially true in today's society.

Challenges May Include:

*Loneliness and unexpected peer pressure

*Difficulty in classes

*A roommate that gets high with his or her friends in your child's room every night

*Sexual advances by a professor

*Challenges to morality

*Unhealthy hazing being required by a fraternity or sorority

*Not making the dance team as expected

*Not wanting to join ROTC, but feeling they must in order to help with tuition

*An unexpected struggle with Opioids

Your student's identity is still being formed and that which has been formed will usually be challenged. You need to stay in relationship with them as never before. You need to know what they are facing.

So often, at a freshman orientation, I convey this to parents. However, all too often they feel like they are trespassing if they ask questions regarding their student's wellbeing.

Due to our counseling center being in a university town, I counsel college student daily. Only God knows what many go through, Higher education is to be a great experience. However, your student needs you for it to be great.

#10 *Act on Red Flags*

As parents, we have to be assertive and honest. If we see something that is not right, we need to act. We need to error on the side of caution.

*If a coach hits your son hard on the helmet during a game in public view, he probably is hitting him more in practice.

*If your 4-year-old-son has teeth marks on his arm and you were not told by your daycare, there is probably more that they are hiding.

*If your 5th grader is afraid to go to school, there is probably a reason.

*If grandad has Lyme's Disease from not taking precautions in his camping and laughs about protection, it probably is not a good idea to let him take your child camping.

*If you know that your neighbor who seems like a nice guy struggles with anger, do not let your children be with him alone.

*A classmate of your son or daughter who tried to get them to watch porn with them says that he didn't mean anything by it. He needs to be monitored.

*If your child seems depressed and is angry and out of character, even if he says that nothing is wrong, there probably is.

This is the list that goes on and on and on, red flags stand out for a reason. They need to be taken seriously. As a fever or physical pain is a sign that something needs to be addressed, so it is with the emotional well-being of your child. It will usually not just go away.

Men are notorious for not going to the doctor when in pain. We will just tough it out. Many times, harm is done due to this mindset. We cannot have this mindset when our children are at stake.

Harmful situations usually just do not go away. They need to be dealt with proactively unto solutions. In this mindset, you make them cease. This is our responsibility as parents and causes our children to feel secure.

I cannot tell you how many times that a junior high or high school student says "I can't believe that dad and mom let me go out on a date with him. What were they thinking? Didn't they see my concern? Why didn't they stand up for me?"

Red flags need to be correlated with you and I standing up, not sitting down.

#11 *Utilization of Technology*

Technological advances are increasing and increasing. In the area of safety, they certainly can be used for good or for wrong. Security systems are a good example of this. They can be used to lock doors to your house or pool. They can be used in regard to surveillance regarding people breaking into your house. As well, they can monitor activity when children are being babysat.

Technological devices now enable you to control the top speed that your child can be driving at. They also can help you set parameters regarding Facebook and cell phone usage. Using this technology does not mean that you do not trust, it is simply a way to gently monitor and set parameters.

Technology can not cause your child's nose to grow 3 inches every time they do something wrong so they will stop. However, it can be a vehicle of safety when utilized properly.

#12 *Truth Keys – Love Keys*

Truth keys -Love keys are simply information given to your children by you in a relational fashion. This informational paradigm is simple and is most effective when established at a young age. However, it can be a great benefit at any age. Children will obtain information one way or another. Why not get it from you?

Too often we let others who have wrong motives influence our children. Consequently, violence and hurtful mindsets are introduced to our children from a young age.

The minds of our children are indeed impressionable. The souls of our children are so soft and penetrable. Herein, we need to guard them and convey input that will facilitate growth and strength. The age graph and correlative information chart below is a guide to help you in this endeavor.

It is not meant to be all inclusive. It is simply a guide to help you to know when to introduce certain information (truth keys). As you present these truth keys in an affirming manner, they will serve as a foundation that can be built upon during their development.

As you share the information, I encourage you to foster an atmosphere of dialogue and education. Your children not only need the truth keys that you have. Inside, they are being changed because they know that you are sharing with them because of the love that you have for them.

Age Graph and Correlative Information

Age	Truth Keys:	Love Keys:		Comments on each stage:
0-3	**Truth Key:** always hold my hand when we are in the parking lot	**Verbal Affirmations:** you are so smart you are so beautiful you are so handsome mommy & daddy love you	**Physical Touch:** hug when celebrating a birthday hug after a fall	be proactive do not wait for the "terrible twos" initiate interaction
4-6	**Truth Keys:** categorize good and bad as putting away toys vs. throwing them saying I love you vs. I hate you hugging someone vs. hitting someone **Unto:** good secrets vs. bad secrets ok places to be touched vs. not ok places to be touched i.e. handshake	**Verbal Affirmations:** I appreciate what you did what you did really helped me what you did really made us proud of you	**Physical Touch:** hold hand when crossing street, in crowd hugs are appropriate	**Example** – every Saturday before lunch, share truth keys with a family game day, a truth key can include a spiritual dimension as well. i.e. God Loves You Unfortunately, at this age the truths of appropriate touch have to be introduced because of the high percentage of sexual abuse occurring during this age period.

	Truth Keys:	Verbal Affirmations:	Physical Touch:	Information:
7-9	bullying sexual abuse opioid abuse i.e. if offered pills	**Information of Success:** when you work hard, great things can happen / look what you can do now stories of success i.e. at your age when Dr. Smith started to read lots of books.... Incorporate encouraging sayings, your own positive experiences	hugs are good	expanded in the context of good and bad and hurtful and helpful
10-12	**Truth Keys:** introduce truths regarding your world view on relationships in general & dating share truths of what a wrong mindset is regarding sexuality stress right and wrong peer relationships in a strong way give success stories regarding those of their age who have helped someone in need,	**Verbal Affirmations:** we appreciate the way you are maturing we appreciate the decisions you are making	**Physical Touch:** hugs are appropriate	**Information:** give information on that which is harmful in a stronger way

13-15	Truth Keys:	Verbal Affirmations:	Physical Touch:	Information:
	share information regarding physical and emotional development	that was a difficult decision, we appreciate how you thought it through	Hugs are still good	again, increase sharing in all areas discussed so far.
	share information correlative to their giftings and interests so they can cultivate their giftings.	your decision helped your friend make a good decision		
	strengthen the truths of low tolerance regarding bullying, abuse, opioids, and sexual assault			
	how to deal with emotions			
	how to choose good friends and be a good friend			
	share statistically of trends good and bad and how it can affect them			
	continue to Affirm I a Big Way!			
16-18	Truth Key:	Verbal Affirmations:	Physical Touch:	Information:
	Information relating to opioids, sexual assault, and bullying needs to continue to be shared.	affirmation & support in all ways is especially needed	hugs are still good	this is a time where specific information needs to be conveyed in a very assertive but loving fashion.
	However, new ways to help others is to be presented	it is time to affirm their interactions in school activities and present		now is the time to present information about post education

	Peer selection is especially targeted through information, youth group interaction can be presented and encouraged.	opportunities for them to be role models to others. affirming good peer selection should be given		aspirations. For example: your daughter thinking about the military is to be presented positive, but the truth that 25,000 accusations of sexual assault in the military took place in 2016 alone.
19-21	**Truth Keys:** *You will face things that you have never faced before we are here for you	**Verbal Affirmations:** You are making us so proud Your future is incredibly bright	**Physical Touch:** hugs are always good	

#13 *Boundaries*

It is imperative that throughout the development of your child that you set boundaries for them. They will accept your boundaries more readily than you think when they are coupled with love, affirmation, and truth.

The boundaries or rules should relate to every category of life in the context of safety. They include morality, relationships, sexuality, learning, respect, work ethic, appreciation, interests, diet, and so much more.

#14 Sixth Grade Proms

There is a push in society today to minimize childhood development. One is seen as immature and lacking if you don't dress and interact in a certain way in 6th grade.

Recently, I dealt with a number of students who were experiencing anxiety due to their approaching 6th grade prom.

Some were struggling emotionally because they were not asked to it by someone (you could still go in a group) others were struggling because they felt pressured to engage in oral sex in regard to the event.

Unfortunately, this can be reality in today's society. Others felt depressed because mom (a single mom) and other parents had a hard time finding the money to buy their gown, accessories and pay for their hair appointment.

Here is a wisdom key – stop it! No child in sixth grade should have to endure making decisions relative to this so-called prom. They will tell you that Mary's mom and dad spent $200 on her and they trust her. Why can't you be like her parents! This is the time for a teachable moment. However, this scenario should already have been dealt with via boundaries prior to the prom becoming an issue.

You as a parent decide when dating is appropriate. It is all about the truth of readiness. Society does not care about whether your child is ready for a prom. They want the $200 your child will spend on the prom; even more appalling is that they want to determine the boundaries for your children rather than you.

#15 Cell Phone

Just this past week, I was involved in a situation where a third grader in a good elementary school was pressured by four other third graders in the restroom to watch a video that they all had on their cell phone. The video was very violent and had to do with an individual contemplating suicide (you can't make this stuff up).

The little boy being pressured was bullied into watching the video. Thankfully, he told his mom who contacted the principal. Parents need to set boundaries according to age readiness regarding cell phones and determine what can and cannot be viewed.

From Facebook and Snapchat to violent gaming and inappropriate movies, boundaries need to be set. In regard to these boundaries, parents need to share their hearts with their children. They do not need Snapchat as much as they need parents that love them enough to say no.

As shared in our introduction, boundaries are to be presented in a positive way. They are to enter into an understanding that in every area of life boundaries are to be respected for their benefit.

#16 *Scenarios*

This is a very simple technique designed to develop a proactive mindset verses a reactive mindset. Many children have never been taught to think before acting. As a result, they simply react emotionally rather than thinking about the consequences of their actions. Under the wisdom key of scenarios, you as a parent do 3 things.

First, you present a real-life scenario that is age appropriate that your child will probably encounter. Second, you ask him or her how they would deal with the scenario presented. Lastly, you dialogue around the answer given.

The answer may deserve immediate affirmation or an opportunity to give alternatives to help. It is an exercise to see where your child is at, to understand him or her, to love and strengthen them.

Example – 5ᵗʰ grader: *If you were asked by your two best friends to smoke a cigarette what would you do?

Example – 9ᵗʰ grader: *If you were in a situation where you were asked by a bully to do his homework for him or get beat up, what would you do? His body language and hesitation may convey a lot. It may be an open door to build relationship and strengthen him.

Example – 11ᵗʰ grader: *Your friend from youth group asks you to the junior-senior prom. He seems like a nice guy. However, just a week before the prom, he says that he will cancel unless you engage in sexual activity with him. How would this affect you?

She may share that she actually expected this because nothing ever goes right for her and that it would just deepen the depression that you knew nothing about. Again, it is an open door not to see her as inferior but as a precious young lady crying out for help.

Example 22 – male, senior in college: *All of your friends are getting engaged to be married. You have no possibilities of relationship at this present time. How does this make you feel?

Scenarios are a simple way to address issues heart to heart proactively. It is simple, but I have seen it be the difference between life and death.

I have seen this wisdom key change so many lives. Children want interaction, they want to convey what they are going through. Scenarios enable them to do this. Initially, it is good to present the scenarios. However, it is also good to let your children be involved in choosing the scenarios as well.

#17 Role Play

Role play is acting out possible scenarios that your child will face. It is that which causes the scenario wisdom key to be accentuated for different children. When a child is literally involved in acting out a situation, it registers on his mind in a strong way. As a parent, or parents, you yourself should definitely be involved in the role play.

You certainly can include siblings as appropriate. As well, you can involve significant others such as relatives or friends of your child as given permission and appropriate.

Role Play Non-Scripted

Example – 5-year-old: *Mommy plays herself – she is in the kitchen, child is in the living room close to the door. Dad tells child that he is playing a stranger knocking at the screen door. Role play is now played out. What does your child do? Does he answer the door? Does he let the stranger in? Does he go to the car with the stranger when told there is a surprise for him?

*The key is teaching the child what is right after he makes his decision. This type of role play is based on unscripted action.

Role Play Scripted

The second type of role play is scripted. This is where the parents go over the right way to act and then role play according to what has been told. Both types of role play are valuable.

Role Play Non-Scripted

Example 9-year-old: Dad and 11-year-old brother play the two friends who assertively try to make your 9-year-old watch a bad video (violent) prior to school starting. Again, after he reacts during this scenario, advice and direction are given.

Role Play Scripted

Prior to the same scenario, advice and directives are shared and then implemented in the scenario.

Role Play Unscripted

Example 14-year-old: Mom plays the friend calling her daughter on cell phone endeavoring to get her to go to a party with her, where drugs and alcohol will be present. The friend appeals to her daughter's friendship conveying that if she is with her, she will not be bad.

However, if she does not go with her, she will probably do wrong things and hurt herself. The daughter plays herself. In this scenario. Due to the age of the child, suggestions can be shared after the role play is done. However, a scripted role play is not usually necessary.

Role Play Unscripted

Example 16-year-old son or daughter: Mom and Dad play two friends on their child's basketball team. One of the friends hurts their back during practice. Later that night, they come over to the house. They know that your mom has OxyContin pills in her cabinet. The friend in pain assertively asks for your child just to give them 2 pills. The big game is tomorrow. He just needs two pills now.

During the role play, observe body language, the degree of hesitation in decision making and possible anxiety in their interaction.

Again, role play is very powerful in its ability to register long term in regard to decision making. It also cultivates expression in your child. It causes your son or daughter to be ready for real life situations. This is due to the reality of them having already acted out the answers.

As well, it makes it easier for your child to come to you when they are facing a difficult situation. This is because they are familiar with interacting with you regarding challenging situations.

#18 *Super Visuals*

Most of us in America are familiar with the Super Bowl. The word super conveys something that stands out. This is key to super visuals. First, what we see certainty impacts us. Referring to the super bowl again, it is typical to pay up to 6 million dollars for a 30 second commercial.

This is obviously due to the impact that the commercial is able to resonate with the viewer. The images presented, and the message associated with the images will cause the viewer to respond proactively. You have heard the expression that a picture is worth a thousand words. This is certainly true.

Personally, there are two pictures that come to mind that have impacted me much over time. The first is a visual that I saw in a driver's education class my senior year in high school.

The movie showed a man thinking about passing in a no passing zone due to a slow-moving car ahead of him. It then showed him making a decision to pass and then him dying. It then showed a grieving family.

I cannot tell you how many times that picture has come to my mind when I think of passing when I know I should not. Even to this day, it impacts me.

The other picture that sticks in my mind is one of my mother. She, with tears running down her face asked me to make a pledge to her that I would never get involved in drugs.

Several of my friends were involved in drugs. One friend, in particular who was a dealer was always trying to get me to try something. Unfortunately, he died due to drug involvement.

I will never forget looking into her big brown eyes as she made this request. It was a request that I fully honored.

Whenever temptation arose, the image of her face gave me strength to do right and still does. Herein, pictures can create caution due to a fear of harm. They also can create motivation for us to do our best.

The following are examples of both. Regarding smoking cigarettes, a picture showing the lungs of a non-smoker as compared to a smoker is a very powerful image. The difference is truly dramatic and accordingly saves lives.

Similar to this picture are pictures of someone using heroin as opposed to a non-user. The brain chemistry of the addict is significantly compromised compared to the brain of the non-user. The pictures again dramatically speak for themselves.

As well, other pictures showing the effects of Opioid abuse can be telling. Whether it is a picture of a teenager in a casket, an emancipated addict with a needle in their arm or a grieving mom, it can be a deterrent to death.

One might think that pictures like this are too much. However, when one sees the profound pain of grieving parents, then you think again. The key is how you present the pictures. It has to be done with compassion and hope. As shared prior, pictures of love and success are to be motivators as well.

A friend of mine has a picture of his brother in his office. His brother was abused by a man in his childhood and used drugs for many years to mask his pain. However, he is now clean and is an awesome counselor in a rehab clinic. My friend uses the picture of his brother as a source of inspiration.

In counseling a while ago, I was counseling a young doctor. To be quite honest, he was having a pity party for himself. He simply was not being thankful, letting little things bother him.

I showed him a picture of a young boy with one arm playing basketball. It touched him. The next session, he brought in a wallet size picture of Jesus being whipped prior to Him going to the cross. He said that he would refer to it when he was feeling sorry for himself. It has worked well for him. Pictures are truly powerful.

I am involved in counseling those who have been sexually abused almost daily and have been for over 35 years. Many times, a victim of abuse struggles with false guilt, even though it is completely untrue.

In this context, I was counseling a young man who continued to condemn himself for what had happened to him, even though he was only six years old at the time.

I was seemingly not making much progress, so I brought in a picture. It was a picture of a little boy's hand at six years of age. When he saw how small it was, he just broke. The picture exemplified in such a strong way how he was not in any way responsible for what had happened.

In another session with a young teenage girl who was very rebellious, I shared with her about the pain she was causing her single mom. However, it didn't seem to register. The next session, I showed her two pictures. One was a picture of someone with a hand that had been burnt. She showed concern and was affected by it. I then showed her a picture of a woman representing her mom who was crying profusely due to emotional pain.

Then I asked her who was in the most pain. She began to weep, and it was the beginning of restoration with her mom and a character change in her. Pictures are a powerful tool. They can sometimes do what words cannot.

#19 *Super Analogies and Quotes*

In themselves, words are very powerful. They have the ability to cause us to enter into the reality of what they represent. Herein, analogies and quotes can be that which causes your child to understand that which you are trying to communicate. As with most all of the wisdom keys, the analogies and quotes are given to be age appropriate.

Examples/ Analogies and Quotes

Young Children:

*I like being with you more than anything

*I love you this much (spread your arms out as much as possible)

*You are Daddy's little princess

*You are smarter than anyone I know

*You are going to be as strong as Superman or Super girl

4th Grade to 6th Grade (ages 9-12)::

*In regard to teaching zero tolerance regarding drugs:

-Just like you can never run out in front of a speeding car, you cannot do drugs ever

-Just like you can never jump off a bridge you can never get involved with drugs

This will usually spark discussion. This will give you the opportunity to explain the facts regarding the harmfulness of drugs, possibility of immediate addiction and other ramifications. If your child does not ask questions leading to discussion, then it will be good for you to elaborate and promote discussion.

Example – Bullying: No person is better than another, no person is made to be hurt by another, no person should ever be bullied!

You have heard people say that sticks and stones can break my bones, but names can never hurt me. This is not true. In fact, getting called bad and hurtful names can hurt more than being hit.

Ages 13-15 years old:

Example – Encouragement:

*The effort you are making will pay off!

*I am proud of you not only for what you do, but who you are!

*When you feel weak you are strong within!

Example – Zero Tolerance:

*Reiterate analogies and talk about those peers who are being successful and those who are not.

Ages 16-18 years old:

*Continue to reiterate truth regarding major areas of harm.

*Continue to use real life examples of those who are succeeding and why, and those who are struggling and why.

Example – Perseverance:

*When the going gets tough, the tough get going; perseverance causes character that can never be taken away.

Example – Relationships:

*It is better to wait for a right relationship than to be scarred by a bad one

*Love is not love until you have to pay a price for the one you love

*Love never fails

*True love causes one to perceive another in an amazing way

*Love is the willingness to wait

Example – Future:

*Your future is as bright as the smile that God gave you. As you have worked so hard, your future will reward you. You are well prepared for tomorrow. In this age bracket and older, expression is very significant. This is due to the ability of your child at this time to put on masks to hide hurt and struggle. The examples given are simply samples. They are to elicit your knowledge and creativity.

*It is amazing how one analogy or one expression can encourage your child. In you as a parent is creativity that needs to be expressed. Herein, you may come up with analogies and thoughts that no one else ever has. As well, you know your children better than anyone else. Consequently, you can put things in a way that they truly relate to.

#20 *Unconditional Love*

Unconditional love is not turning a blind eye to behaviors in your child that need worked on. Unconditional love is real love. It is a love that causes a parent to first love their child for who they are and not for what they do. It is a love that causes a parent to see the glory of the real them even when they might be struggling.

It is a love that can never have a favorite child. This is because the glory within each child is equally amazing. Unfortunately, in today's society, conditional love is increasingly the norm. Parents come to the game if their child is starting. A child is given more value if they obtain first place rather than second even if they did their best.

Unconditional love enables a child to establish their identity. They become satisfied with who they are. They are at rest. This is a key that you cannot live without as a parent. The following are ways that will help you love unconditionally and communicate it to your child.

*Experience the reality of unconditional love yourself. You cannot give what you do not have. This reality can come from God, your own parents and from those that you associate with. Being loved unconditionally does not mean you are with people that do not confront your wrong doings. It is being with people who put you even above themselves in their desire to see you succeed.

*Teach your children from a young age the characteristics of unconditional love.

*Verbalize to them that they light up your life simply by being who they are.

*Every person alive has their unique and individualized set of fingerprints. Accordingly, your child alone has the innate ability to touch your heart as no one else can, in a unique & special way.

*Live the life. Let your expressions speak for you. Parents, it is ok to look at your son in 6th grade on a normal day when he smiles and shed a few tears. When he asks you why you are crying, tell him it's just because he is amazing.

*Parents, when your 8th grade daughter spends 2 hours on her hair, make-up, and dress before school, let those tears flow as well! When she asks you why you are crying, tell her why. It is because you look amazing and there is no one in your eyes that will ever be more beautiful than her.

*Live the life by your actions. If your son or daughter is going through a difficult time, do not change your attitude of esteem regarding them. It might be them struggling with being a little too hyper in first grade or struggling with reading in third grade. It might be them getting detention in 7th grade and yelling back at you in 10th grade. You might have to show some tough love but never either be inconvenienced by them or see them any differently.

   Some things are taught, and some things are caught. Unconditional love goes beyond the outward. It comes from the heart and goes into the heart. It is what causes you to be who you are to them. It is what causes them to have hope and want to be like you.

#21 *Parent Intuition*

Some things are easily understood, some things are not. It is just a heart thing, there are times when you as a mom or dad just sense something is not right. You just sense in your heart, in your gut that they should not be with this person or go to this place. It is not an everyday occurrence. However, when it does occur, it is wisdom to pay attention to that something.

A young mom of a preschooler was going to drop her son off at her aunt's house. However, she just didn't feel right about it. She called her aunt and just said she couldn't drop her son off today. Later, she found out that a team of men were replacing her windows and one of the men could have caused the environment to be unsafe. You are not to be obsessive, but that something many call parental intuition can be an asset.

#22 *Support Activities*

It is wisdom not to do everything alone, but to take advantage of activities and groups that can augment your quest for safety. It is helpful at all ages. It can be especially helpful when your child needs to hear things from others that he respects.

Sliver Ring Thing

Sliver Ring Thing is an event that promotes abstinence before marriage and general character for our youth. Many of the events attract over 5,000 youth and are held in local communities. They incorporate speakers that speak the language of today and employ great contemporary music. The response of the youth is amazing.

Big Brothers – Big Sisters

If you are a single mom, this can be an avenue of blessing. A reputable individual simply will spend time with your child intermittently as your desire them too.

My cousin Joe, who was a pharmacist in Virginia was a Big Brother. He was married with 2 children of his own, but just wanted to help. His sponsored little brother benefitted much from their interaction.

Boy Scouts – Girl Scouts

Most are aware of these organizations. This group can be a source of positive interaction for your child.

Father-Daughter Valentine Dance

This activity is becoming increasingly popular in many local communities. It is usually for children 11 years and under. It is a special time of fun and affirmation.

Camps

There are some camps that are imply amazing regarding reinforcing values and cultivating character in an atmosphere of fun. *Summers Best*, two weeks in western Pennsylvania is just one of hundreds that can be of great benefit to your child.

Church Youth Groups

From groups for the very young such as Awana to high school youth groups, this can be an invaluable resource for your child. It is a place where positive peer relationships can be found and cultivated. As well, it is a safe environment where children can grow regarding their character.

#23 *Peer Evaluation*

You are not called to micro mange your children. However, you are called to be a fruit inspector. Those that your children befriend will determine much regarding the safety of your child. Consequently, it is very important to keep an eye out regarding who your children are associated with.

This goes from first grade to college. Decisions determine destiny. One of the major decisions that parents and children alike make is in regard to relationship. Wholesome relationships will include the following attributes.

*Relationships that promote foundational morality and do not diminish it.

*Relationships that are not one sided, where one party takes precedence over another. This one sidedness can be in the context of one being the center of attention, always needing the other party to help them with an emotional need or always getting their own way.

*Relationships that do not cause the other to minimize priorities such as studying, hard work, family, and helping others, but promotes these areas.

*Relationships that encourage interaction with others of good character and right motive.

These attributes of relationship should be taught at an early age and consistently be reiterated. Likewise, dad and mom, you have to always be observant in this area. Even a good friend in 7th grade can turn out to be very detrimental in 9th grade.

From an early age, due to the importance of this area, your children need to know that their associations will always be of a primary concern due to your love for them. This is not micro managing or negative interference. It is parental responsibility and love.

#24 *Scale of 1to 10 how are you doing? *

This wisdom key is very simple. It is simply eliciting verbal communication regarding how things are going. For a younger child, you do not have to use the one to ten scale. (ten being the best). You can just ask how they are doing. How was preschool or kindergarten today? However, as children get older, the scale is good because it causes them to evaluate themselves.

All too often, our children struggle, and they do not realize the degree of the struggle. Herein, it is important that they learn to discern times of difficulty. One cannot adequately problem solve if they do not realize a problem exists. We all realize that teen suicide continues to rise. One variable of prevention is helping our children to self-evaluate.

Obviously, this simple question of how you are doing also helps us as parents evaluate as well. In our busy schedule, it is easy for this simple question never to be consistently asked. Children at times may not seem like they want you to ask them about their day. However, they do!

This is why it is so important to spend time with your child where you can discuss things. This can happen by taking your child fishing, just you and him or her. It can be going to Starbucks or a special restaurant for a mother-daughter time. The feedback we get back as parents regarding this simple wisdom key is amazing to me.

Parents are usually surprised regarding what their children shared. They really were not aware of how much a friend moving away impacted their daughter. They were not aware of how much pressure they were under regarding the Sadie Hawkins dance.

I have had dads communicate that until they went out to breakfast with their son, that they had no idea that his son was struggling with suicidal thoughts. We are living in a time that never has existed before regarding what our children face. They are desiring, that we as parents enter into their world, even though they may say otherwise at times.

#25 *Honest Expression of Emotions*

It is imperative that we understand how much our children need to express their emotions. Emotions that are not expressed and become penned up will usually at some point in time be expressed in a detrimental fashion. The following counseling situation that took place years ago exemplifies this.

This individual who is married now often shares this and has allowed me to do so as well. This young man was very close to both of his parents, he and his mother had a very special bond. He was a very good athlete and she came to all his sporting events. Unfortunately, she was diagnosed with cancer and at the end of his junior year in high school, she died.

This young man was overwhelmed with the loss but grieved little. This is because he and his brothers were taught that this was indicative of strength. Towards the end of his senior year until the beginning of his sophomore year in college, he struggled much emotionally and with doing wrong things.

To complicate matters, his dad, a good and faithful man quickly married after the death of his wife. To make a long story short, at one of our initial counseling sessions, he broke down. I never heard anyone weep as he did.

He wept and wept for almost an hour. This was not weakness, it was wisdom and strength. It is interesting to note that even Jesus wept. There is a balance, we do need to get over things. However, we need to process events of pain and not deny the impact that they have on us. Consequently, we need to express our grief.

Divorce can have a strong impact on our children, young and older. We need let them process in a way that their honest emotions can be communicated.

Both dads and moms need to learn to laugh and to cry with their children. However, this can be difficult if our own parents did not express emotions to us or if we have been taught that the showing of emotion is a sign of weakness.

A friend of mine shared of how God had helped him while speaking in front of the church. As he did, he cried quite profusely. On the way to the parking lot, I walked out with him and his 5-year-old son and 4-year-old nephew. The nephew who had been taught that crying is bad, asked his uncle why he cried in church. The uncle responded by saying that Jesus in his heart caused him to cry. His little nephew responded by saying, "Jesus, get out of my uncle's heart!"

We need to see that emotions are a key to expression for our good and the good of others. It is important to note that this wisdom key is not titled, the expression of emotion, but the honest expression of emotions. This is significant in that honesty is very significant. This is because in our hearts, many times we have an honest need to express our emotions but minimize this need.

Men are especially vulnerable regarding minimizing things. This includes the need for expression or the time that it takes for one to process pain. This can be detrimental in a marriage and in child rearing. A man can yell at his wife at six o'clock and because he is genuinely sorry expects his wife to forget about it by eight o'clock. This is because he has! He then thinks his wife is wrong by still being affected by it. This not wisdom!

Wisdom is understanding that forgiveness is immediate, but harsh words can produce hurt that takes some time to mend. Again, there is a balance in the context of time but does not negate the reality of time being necessary for mending to take place. Sometimes, we as men do not even realize that we are minimizing reality.

Years ago, my daughter was playing varsity basketball and hurt her finger. She had to be taken out of the game and we went to an orthopedic surgeon the next day. He examined her and came to the following conclusion; her finger is slightly fractured, but she can play the rest of the season. After getting in the car, I responded happily by saying that this was great news and that she was going to have a great season!

She responded by saying the following, "What! You are happy that I am going to walk down the aisle on my wedding day with a crooked finger?!" She was honest, and we had a good conversation a day later after she calmed down. She did have a good season and I did learn a great lesson. I had expected her to respond like me and minimize the situation, especially in light of her ability to play. I did not even consider that there was another perspective. Obviously, there was.

What if my daughter did not feel the freedom to convey her perspective? First, I would have been wrong by not considering her perspective and not even know it. She could have misperceived my response as selfish as opposed to my being happy for her. This could have resulted in a misperception of me. When there is not honest dialogue and honest expression of emotions with our children or others, there will be an open door to misperception.

Daddy and mommy could not come to my science fair when I won first place, due to business commitments. However, two days later they went to my brother's soccer game. I told them that I understood, but I really don't. Do not assume that when your child says that they understand, that they really do. Take time to make sure that they really do understand.

To the man who is reading this text, here is a wisdom tip for you. When you are in the car and you ask your wife where she wants to go to eat, she will usually say that she doesn't care where you go. Then when you pick a place (usually a place where there are multiple television screens with sporting events), you wonder why she is not happy. When she said that she doesn't care where you eat, she is really saying, do you care enough about me to ask me again, so I can really tell you? It is important to really want to see what others are really saying!

#26*The Power of Prayer*

I would be amiss if I did not include this variable in the wisdom keys of safety. Millions of people in America worldwide believe in prayer regarding safety. I hear stories from people of all walks of life who attribute their being unharmed or alive today to prayer.

It is interesting that the majority of stories communicated to me revolve around a particular Psalm in the Old Testament. I know of both those of a Jewish persuasion and those of a Christian persuasion who pray utilizing this Psalm daily.

Psalm 91

"He that dwelleth in the secret place of the
most High shall abide under
the shadow of the Almighty. I will say of the
Lord, He is my refuge and
my fortress; my God; in him will I trust.
Surely he shall deliver thee from
the snare of the fowler, and from the noisome
pestilence. He shall cover
thee with his feathers, and under his wings
shalt thou trust: his truth shall
be they shield and buckler. Thou shalt not be
afraid for the terror by night;
nor the arrow that flieth by day; Nor for
the pestilence that walketh in
darkness; nor for the destruction that wasteth
at noonday. A thousand shall
fall at thy side, and ten thousand at thy right
hand; but it shall not come nigh thee.
Only with thine eyes shalt thou behold and see the
eward of the wicked.
Because thou hast made the Lord, which is my
refuge, even the most High,
thy habitation; There shall no evil befall thee,
neither shall any plague come
nigh thy dwelling. For he shall give his angels charge

over thee, to keep thee in all thy ways.
They shall bear thee up in their hands, lest thou
dash thy foot against
a stone. Thou shalt tread upon the lion and
adder: the young lion and the dragon
shat thou trample under feet. Because he hath
set his love upon me, therefore
will I deliver him: I will set him on high, because
he hath known my name. He shall
call upon me, and I will answer him; I will be
with him in trouble; I will deliver him, and
honour him. With long life will I satisfy him,
and shew him my salvation."

The affinity that exists between the person praying and this Psalm itself is almost overwhelming. This affinity seems to exist due to three reasons. First it is very personal. It is filled with a relational tone that causes the reader to be easily entreated. Second, it is filled with an emotional chord of concern. It is God communicating that He truly understands our great concern regarding our need to be safe.

In our initial chapter, we shared that wisdom is making the main thing the main thing. Many times, individuals feel a disconnect between God and their present situations. This Psalm is the antithesis of this reality.

This Psalm conveys a God who connects with us regarding that which is most important to us. Compassion and connection seem to flow through the words of this Psalm. It connects the reader to God in a way that is very relatable. As a result, there is drawing effect that causes one to be able to feel that these words apply to him or her personally.

Lastly, intrinsic to the Psalm is a decisiveness that permeates all that is conveyed. In this one Psalm, no less than 7 times is the expression "*I will*" used by God. It is obvious that the scripture is communicating God's will through this repetition. Regarding all those that I have talked to regarding their stories, this is that which they usually emphasize.

It is a sense of confidence that they ascribe to the strength of the Psalm. Psalm 91 does not discount the reality of their being evil and trouble in our midst. It simply offers provision in the environment that we find ourselves in.

The provision causes hope to rise up within us, hope is indeed so very necessary as it protects our mind. It acts as a buffer between struggle and possible harm. Hope is so very powerful in that it keeps us connected with a positive attitude and goodness.

To many the principles intrinsic to this text, if adhered to will seemingly increase the probability of your child or children being kept safe.

However, the principles conveyed in this Psalm are certainty not all inclusive. As well, as parents, we are not perfect, and we have our limitations. This does not mean that we are not responsible and accountable for our actions.

We should passionately do all that we can and know to do. However, it is good to know that through our faith that God has our back. As we do what we can do, Psalm 91 communicates the reality that He will do that which we can't.

I remember years ago an experience that I had when I taught high school age students at a youth development center in Pennsylvania. The students had all committed felonies and 3 students in my one class had committed murder. I claimed Psalm 91 daily and that God would protect me via his favor. I could tell that one of the boys was up to no good and shared it with my supervisor.

He actually shared that he was going to hurt someone and break out. However, when he said this, he looked at me and said the following, "For some reason, I could never take you out because … I just can't". A week later, he hurt an overnight staff guy and tried to break out. Thankfully, the man survived; all that I know is that I did everything that I was responsible to do to ensure my safety.

However, God seemed to confirm Psalm 91 in having my back. I believe that the need for faith is not a weakness, but wisdom that gives us strength. Truly, in our endeavor to keep our children safe, strength is at a premium.

#27 *Involvement on this Issue*

Your reading this book is an indication of true concern for your child or children. More likely than not, your concern for your own flows over to a concern for others. Herein, as time permits, and you feel comfortable, your involvement with issues of safety could benefit others and you as well. More often than not, we minimize ourselves in regard to the impact that we can have on others. However, we can have a great impact.

The following are some ways that you can become involved in the issues of safety, as you feel comfortable.

*Due to so many of the safety issues being so prevalent, virtually everyone is affected in some way.

Due to this reality, you will be involved with people in your sphere of influence who are desiring one or two things. These things are a desire to be more equipped regarding their own children regarding prevention or help involving a situation that they are now having to deal with.

Regarding prevention, you can share with them some of keys that you have learned. You can encourage them and offer them materials and resources.

You may be surprised how this can help someone. As well, often times, individuals open up and share their concerns when they simply know that you care.

In regard to those who are dealing with a child who is in a crisis situation, you can be a point of contact to help them as well. For example, if their child is being bullied, or fighting an addiction or depression, you can help them in two ways.

You can refer them to an appropriate place to obtain help (you will have to have a list of appropriate options) and you can simply offer encouragement and hope. There are so many that are dealing with issues.

Five years ago, when a forum on Opioid abuse was announced to the community, maybe a dozen people would show up. Now, hundreds show up. People are looking for answers in the area of prevention and present crisis. You may be the answer to someone's need.

*You may have an idea or a recommendation that would really make a difference in your school or community.

Accordingly, get involved as a community member at large on the safety committee of the school board or simply share your recommendations with the committee. As one being involved with local school boards on the safety committee, I can assure you that your suggestions will be appreciated.

*You can be a catalyst to informing people of what is going on and how to proactively combat these challenges.

You can do this through helping set up seminars or forums through a community group like the rotary or a local church. For example, our counseling center has those specifically designated to help in this area. The response and the positive results from the seminars exceeded our own expectations.

*Most organizations like Big Brothers – Big Sisters are always in need of volunteers. Whether working directly with a child or helping in the office, your contribution is of great valve.

*If you are a person of faith, prayer is usually very important to you. You can utilize prayer in at least three ways.

When you find yourself with someone in crisis regarding their children, you can offer to pray with them. You may be surprised how meaningful this is to those in the midst of challenges. Second, you can pray yourself for God to stem the tide of harm in our country through his wisdom and grace. Third, you can be involved in organizing a prayer service to pray for our nation and to pray specifically for those battling addiction and stress. Churches of all denominations are beginning to reach out in this way.

*Organizations and counseling center are always in need of funds to keep going, I can personally testify to this!

As a result, your participation in a fund-raising event like a walk-a-thon or a banquet can go a long way. Help is always greatly needed in events like this.

*You can always be a voice legislatively. Laws like *Megan's Law* has been a true deterrent to abuse. Many laws like this come into being through grass roots efforts started by concerned parents just like you.

*You may be gifted in regard to having the ability to start a group like *Big Brothers – Big Sisters* or *Celebrate Recovery*. Again, do not underestimate yourself. Where there is a passion for good, there is a way.

*Lastly, you may have a creative idea within you. It may be a billboard with a unique slogan. It may be a specific support group. In my area, unfortunately, 94 individuals lost their lives due to drug overdose. One woman obtained permission to put up crosses in memory of each of them. At the site, which is in the middle of town is a number for help.

This year, the number of deaths has significantly decreased. I think that her act of concern has had something to do with this.

One of the most difficult things about doing seminars and even writing this book is talking with those who have lost children, or who have had children hurt is when they say the following. *If only I had known what you are sharing now prior to my situation, I know that it could have changed things.*

I always try to enter into their hurt and assure them that they have done everything that they knew to do. They are certainly not at fault. Many of these parents, in their children's memory and out of love for others are the greatest vehicles of help in the area of protection. It is incredibly helpful when parents like yourself encourage these parents.

The rationale for involvement in helping others is twofold. The first is obvious, so many people need you! They need your involvement. Whether it is doing some office work, participating in a walk or sharing ideas to help problem solve, your participation is invaluable. Second, it will benefit you in regard to your own household. When you give, it just seems like you receive back in your own life. It is the law of reciprocity. As well, it certainly keeps you on the cutting edge of safety regarding needs and trends.

#28 *Proactive Groups and Relationships*

In our prior wisdom key, the emphasis was on you reaching out to others. In this wisdom key, the emphasis is on others reaching out to you. May times, we do not realize how much we put out in a day or over time. Correspondingly, we need to be filled back up.

As a result, it is so very important to have a venue for this infilling This can be accomplished through a group like MOPS (Mothers of Preschoolers), support groups or just consistently meeting with others who are positive and proactive. These significant others can include friends your age and those older who can act as mentors in your life that you trust.

If you are married your spouse is of course a significant other as well! When you put out day in and day out especially when you are facing challenges, you can feel all alone. Then this alone feeling can cause you to be alone. You can isolate yourself thinking that either nobody else faces what you face or struggles like you do. When you interact with others, you find that they face the same battles and have the same struggles at times.

As well, when you are with others that are positive and proactive, you get strengthened. The key is not being consistently with those who are negative and not proactive. Part of wisdom is knowing that we cannot do everything on our own, that we need others. This is an important truth and a key to relationships. As you are involved in these relationships, you will be able to give to others as well, regarding that which is in you. It is a win-win situation.

#29 *Peace and Joy*

Well, we are at our twenty-ninth wisdom tip! As with anything of value, there are a number of variables involved. The key is to not be overwhelmed by these variables, but to progressively enter into them. Herein, I believe that this last wisdom key will be of help to you.

The following paradigm encapsulates this last key. Doing right causes peace which is then accompanied by joy. This is a simple principle but one that is incredibly important.

No human being is perfect or will ever be. However, when we consistently do the best that we can, good things will take place. In the context of keeping our children safe, we can only do what we can do. We cannot afford to enter into unrealistic expectations. We will forget to put everything in our children's lunch boxes that we should. We may raise our voices at times when we should not.

At times, we may use tough love when we should just give a hug. At times we will give a hug when we should give consequences in the spirit of tough love. It is ok!

You, your spouse and your kids will be just fine! You are not to enter into a perfectionistic attitude always having to do everything just perfectly. As long as you consistently are doing your best to do right, you are sowing rightly. Accordingly, you will reap a harvest.

A farmer cultivates the ground and plants seed. He then does the best he can to enable the seed to grow. He does his best to water the seed, and keep the bugs, and crows away.

As well, if a cold spell comes, if appropriate he may cover the crop for a night or two. However, his job is limited. If he misses a watering time or if his scarecrow falls down for a day (the scarecrow can represent a good dad opening up the door to invite a young man inside who is taking his daughter out on her first date), the seed will still grow. The crop will still flourish.

This is because the seed is unaffected by imperfection. This is due to the seed process having within it, the ability to endure wind and degrees of adversity. Your children desperately need you to do right in their lives. However, they are made in a way, with a resiliently that supersedes our need to do everything 100% right.

This lends itself to peace. Peace is the absence of anxiety and fear due to our knowing that we have done the best we can in a reasonable fashion. Peace is also knowing that although there may be some challenges at times, the seed grows up and turns into harvest.

Peace is indeed a virtue. It is very powerful, in that it causes hope to be resident at all times. It enables one to remain stable even when the wind is blowing hard. As parents, we are not to raise our children in anxiety or fear. We are to raise them in peace.

Doing the best we can translates into peace. Peace translates into joy. Joy is a heart happiness that causes us to enjoy. We enjoy our children due to who they are to us and who we are to them. We enjoy their smiles, their laughter, and their uniqueness.

Their growth in character even through challenges gives us great joy. During each stage of development, we rejoice in their success. Their presence alone in who they are to us, in who they are becoming brings joy that words cannot express. Joy is a gauge of one's strength. When you are in joy and enjoying your children, it provides an atmosphere of growth without undue pressure. When you are doing right which is doing your best, your children pickup on your commitment to them.

It is simply a win-win situation. You are doing the very best that you can to ensure the safety of your children brings peace. This peace enables you to enjoy your children. This in turn enables them to grow up in an environment conducive to growth.

Chapter 5

True Stories

It is so very important to understand that the principles and wisdom keys when implemented will work for you. It is also so very important to understand that you are very able to implement the strategies shared. Intrinsic to the principles, keys and strategies given is a derived sense of confidence. It is my desire that you are completely confident with your ability to use them and in their effectiveness.

Accordingly, in this chapter I am going to share 12 stories of those who have had the same principles and wisdom keys shared with them that you have. In the stories, you will see regular people like yourselves in their weaknesses and struggles help their children grow up strong. In some cases, you will see how parents helped their children overcome incredible odds. The names and places of course have been changed for the sake of anonymity. However, most all have shared their stories repeatedly to the encouragement of others.

Story #1 – Our Need to be Whole

Joe's wife, Tara, came to the center due to her frustration with her husband's refusal to discipline their four-and-a-half-year-old daughter. Joe and Tara had been married for 7 years. Joe is a good guy who has a good job. He likes restoring old cars and esteems his wife and loves his daughter. However, he greatly dislikes confrontation and has great difficulty regarding assertiveness.

Herein, he does not like it when Tara disciples in virtually anyway. This even includes time out. Due to their marriage being affected, Joe came in. He openly shared his philosophy of discipline being cruel. The daughter was definitely being harmed by the disorder in the house. She ate too many sweets which was having a detrimental effect on her teeth. She did not share with other children at all. Most disturbing was her throwing tantrums when she didn't get her own way.

Joe agreed to meet with me by himself. I asked Tara to please be patient, she agreed. On the fourth session, Joe broke down. He shared of being raised primarily by his grandparents for three years. They were extremely strict. He was not allowed to play sports, had to do excessive chores, and was not allowed to have friends over much.

The worst was that he was sexually abused by the step-grandfather every other weekend. This happened over a three-year period when he was 7, 8, and 9 years old. He correlated the abuse with the ultra-strict discipline that he received during the years of harm. Joe went through the *Through His Eyes* program designed for those who have been abused.

Things changed dramatically regarding his mindset about discipline. It took time, but their daughter thankfully did recover. Joe shares with men through his church. His message is simple, but strong. He shares that before you can be who your child and spouse need you to be, you need to do what you need to do to be whole yourself. This is certainly a key in all our lives.

Story #2 – Fast and Slower

David's brother John referred him to the center that I was working with. John's own son had struggled with Heroin for about 5 years, from the age of 17-22. During his five-year struggle, he died twice and was brought back by Narcan. To make a long story short, this nephew was Heroin free after 3 ½ months. That was 4 years ago, and he had never gone back. To be very honest, it usually does not work like that.

David, seeing what he had termed a miracle in his nephew asked me to help his own son. His son, Jerry, was 26 years old when he came to see me. He actually came in with his dad. Jerry was a bright young man. He had been struggling with Heroin for 3 years and had been in 3 rehab centers in the last 2 years. He readily admitted to using at the time we met. To be honest, he was not committed to the process when we first met.

Our center is not a rehab center. Our program deals with root issues that can contribute to the problem. Different times, they will go to a rehab after doing counseling with us. After about a month, Jerry did commit to our program, I believe that he was genuine. He even shared of his hope to be clean with his family. However, to be quite honest, things did not go as well as we had hoped.

After a year, Jerry was in and out of addiction. As a result, his dad came to me in a very angry manner. He accused me of not working with his son like I did with his nephew. This was of course not true, and he later apologized.

In this case it took Jerry almost 2 ½ years before he obtained the consistency correlative to freedom. Even with Jerry's consistency (we are very proud of him) he still attends weekly NA (narcotic anonymous) meetings.

With each of the 10 stories chosen, there is a specific variable emphasized. In this story, the variable of emphasis is time. It is very important that we understand that individuals respond different to the challenges that they face. In this case Jerry's cousin obtained closure in 3 ½ months. Jerry himself took about 2 ½ years, regarding Heroin addiction.

What I want to emphasis is that Jerry tried just as hard as his cousin, but the time frame was different. Now, to balance this equation, commitment and effort are two primary keys. However, there can be other variables involved regarding heroin. Some of the variables involved can be the degree of abuse, different changes in brain chemistry and the support system offered.

Accordingly, we have to understand two things. First, we cannot fully compare one individual with another. Second, we cannot assume that because there is struggle, the person is not trying. If you walked in their shoes, you may not do as well as them.

However, we need to expect results. The way to those results though may be different from one individual to another.

I was working with a very good family a while ago. They had two boys, two years apart. The oldest child was diagnosed with a mild learning disability in first grade. He struggled learning to read. He reversed both letters and numbers in his printing and was frustrated. However, by the end of his 2nd grade school year, he was at the top of his class.

His younger brother was diagnosed in first grade with the exact same type of disability. Although, by the end of his 2nd grade year, he was still struggling in learning to read. His dad was a great guy but grew frustrated with this little boy's lack of progress. This was due to comparing his progress with that of his older brother.

The struggle continued into the middle of his 3rd grade year. It was then that a new school Psychologist suggested the possibility of an eye problem. It turned out that the Psychologist was right. The youngest son had a problem that affected his peripheral vision. After corrected, the youngest son improved dramatically academically.

Again, individuals and situations vary. This effects time frames and strategies. When the process is taking longer than we would like with our children due to these variables, they need our patient support as never before.

Story #3 – You have to Stand Up Now

Bullying can take many forms. From being hit on the playground to being degraded by either verbal abuse or exclusion, it is heart wrenching.

This is because intrinsic to our make-up is the need of affirmation and a vulnerability to pain when dominated wrongly.

Bonnie, at age 11 was very successful. She did great in school, great in gymnastics and had a lot of friends. When she entered high school, her goal was to continue her success academically, in sports, and in peer acceptance. However, she was unexpectanlty challenged by some girls who resented her success. For whatever reason, they targeted her via social media and by verbally spreading rumors about her.

Not being used to having classmates do such a thing, she did not know how to respond. Consequently, she started to withdraw and did not want to go to school. Her parents did not know why she was struggling. They just assumed that it was learning to adapt to a larger school, an unfamiliar environment.

For some reason, she did not disclose what was going on. This was in part due to her being threatened by the girls. I met with the family and in the initial session, she broke down and shared what was happening. Her parents immediately went to the school with Bonnie and shared what was going on. Unfortunately, the administration drug their feet and the bullying continued.

Now this was 4 years ago, and policies were not in place regarding bullying as they are today. However, there still was no excuse for the delay. Here is what I want to get across to you. Dad had a business trip planned but cancelled it. He contacted school board members, talked to the Superintendent and contacted Police.

Some may see this as excessive, but to be honest, if your 9th grade daughter was being bullied, you probably would change your mind. To make a long story short, due to Dad's proactive stance, the group of girls were disciplined, and the bullying stopped.

The dad canceling his trip did 4 things. It stopped the bullying quickly. It caused Bonnie to see her parents step up in order to protect her. It caused Bonnie to see how she could disclose what was going on in life, knowing the benefits of her parents' involvement.

Lastly, it was found out that this group of girls had bullied another girl. This other girl changed schools and is still struggling from the effects of her being bullied in junior high by them, nobody stood up for her.

I do not know the details of the situation, but I do know that in her situation, it was never addressed. As parents, when there is a scenario that is bringing harm to our children, it is not only imperative that we sacrificially stand up but stand up quickly.

Certainly, it is important to get the story right. It is also important not to do something inappropriate and to go through the right channels.

However, we cannot let fear or feeling uncomfortable keep us from standing up for our children. Very simply, they need us to. This should be sufficient motivation in itself.

<u>Story #4 – Learning to Communicate</u>

A mother of five contacted the center due to one of her children having outbursts of anger. She was the youngest at 8 years of age. We met with mom to discuss the situation. It turned out that the situation with the little girl was not as severe as thought. However, as what often happens, another issue of great concern was brought up.

This mom shared of being overwhelmed with having to be the parent that dealt with the children herself; whenever a difficult situation arose. Her other children were 10, 12, 14, and 16. Each of them were facing age appropriate normal challenges. However, one child was fighting a real struggle with alcohol.

To make another long story short, I gave her a brochure on the variable of communication. It contained the same information shared in this text. Consequently, she gave it to her husband. He called me a few days later and was very angry. He conveyed that it was not his style to communicate openly and should not be pressured to do so. He said that he would not come in to talk to me.

I met with the mom and the older children. They all expressed strong disdain for their dad's lack of interaction with them. They saw his lack of communication as uncaring and hurtful. The young man who was struggling with alcohol even called him a coward, wow! The dad was hardworking and a very moral man and did care about his children. However, he truly did come across as uncaring and disinterested.

Finally, the dad agreed to meet with me. I was very direct. I shared of what I thought the children's perceptions were of him. He acted shocked and said nothing but did cry. He then shared that even if he wanted to, he could not express himself as this was not who he was. I simply told him that he could certainly cry at their hurt and say that he loved them, I also shared that he needed to say he was sorry for his being distant.

Well, we all met, and it was very tense. The boy struggling with alcohol broke the ice by asking, "why don't you care about us?" The young 12-year-old girl asked why he didn't love her.

The dad began to weep and said that he loved her and apologized to the older son. Then he apologized to the others. It was heart felt and the mom and kids knew it. We later found out that the 12-year-old had been fighting thoughts of suicide and no one knew it.

I worked with the dad for eight sessions regarding communication skills. The amazing thing is that he actually ended up being quite a talker. His change elicited an amazing change in each of the children. It had a great impact on his marriage as well.

I shared this story to convey the importance of communication. However, I also shared it so that you could see that it is critical to be willing to learn so that we can change as needed for our children.

As a footnote to this story, this dad took his 10-year-old daughter to the Father – Daughter Valentine's Day Dance, sponsored by a community group. A day later, he called me up to tell me how much it meant to his daughter. I couldn't help but shed some tears. He is becoming the dad he was always meant to be.

<u>Story #5 – School Safety</u>

So much has changed regarding going to school. There are many who, as students, face danger due to the present school environment. We have already discussed making it a priority to investigate the school your children will be going to prior to sending them there.

This is true when you are moving into a new area. It is of course true as your children are starting school. Some children may do better in private school and some may do better being homeschooled. Some will do better in a smaller school than a larger school. It is a key to know what is best for them.

I want to share a story revolving around Mr. Elijah Stanton and his wife Tamara. They had two children in a public school. Their older child James was just entering 9th grade and their daughter Jasmin was entering 7th grade. These parents knew that the school system that their children were attending was challenging. Both parents became acquainted with the principles shared in this text through a seminar that they attended.

Due to challenges they knew their children would face, they spent a lot of time with them, especially regarding school safety. They did scenarios and role play, and really developed a close relationship with them. Unfortunately, there was gang violence at the school to some degree. Both Children knew of people who had been harmed.

Three things transpired that I thought was interesting. First, different friends of James and Jasmine came to their house, seeing it as a safe place. Mr. & Mrs. Stanton shared with them in a very personal way. One young man said he went out for football, but really didn't like it. When asked why he played, he said he just felt safe on the field. The kids really opened up and a support group was naturally realized.

Second, those parents asked their Pastor if at Sunday school, they could do a 9 week focus on school safety. To me, that was awesome. Why don't we meet people where they are at? If safety is a need with these kids, why not address it in our communities?

Years ago, a young lady who just graduated from college went to Harlem, New York City. My wife and I were helping her with her desire to help the kids that she was involved with. Many were in an unsafe environment. It was amazing what happened when this issue became a focal point. They were taught how to deal with their environment and it changed their lives.

Lastly, Mr. Stanton was asked by the guidance department to come in during an activity period to work with at risk students. There were about 20 students. He utilized the same principles that he taught his children. I cannot tell you the number of stories that came about through this interaction.

One young man who was in the same class as James shared this. He said, "instead of being someone who would hurt someone like my brother did, I have made a choice to help the situation!" This story is simply shared to show you that when put into practice, the principles truly do work. They work where your children live, play, and go to school.

Not all schools will let someone like Mr. Stanton come in and work with their students. However, school administrators are looking for solutions and do want community involvement as never before.

One of the main reasons that I shared this story is to convey that many students are looking for a safe zone. They are looking for mentors. They are looking for good friends. The Stanton family provided all three of these needs.

Story #6 – Mom is Looking

Cindi is a single mom with two teenagers, Jill 14 and David 16. She is forty-one years old and a great mom. Her husband left her for another woman when the children were 6 and 8 and left the kids as well. Cindi went to a seminar that I held recently. She received much from what was shared. She especially picked up on the wisdom keys relating to peer pressure.

Accordingly, she made a commitment to evaluate the peers of her children to ensure their safety. What to me is so great, is that she went beyond the wisdom keys given to her, utilizing her own creativity. She used our peer evaluation help list (located in back of this text) which includes simple observation, communication, and parallel information.

Cindi, is a supervisor whose job description includes hiring and training of staff. Cindi added 3 extra vehicles of evaluation to help in the area of peers. Now, she was not micromanaging her children in an overbearing manner. She is an amazing mom and her children not only love her but respect her. This is so important because it is not just what you do, but how you do it.

Cindi's added vehicles of evaluation included the utilization of Facebook, a special dinner, and a fun survey. Cindi, in her job utilizes Facebook to discern the quality of the applicants that are trying to obtain a job at her company. This is now part of the normal due process regarding hiring. Herein, one needs to be very careful what their Facebook conveys.

Amazingly, most do not do this. I am on the board of different organizations. Regarding one of the organizations, our director eliminated 9 out of 12 applicants by simply looking at what their Facebook negatively conveyed.

One applicant shared on Facebook that she would never give a full effort work wise if payed under $40,000 a year. She was being offered under $30,000 for filling the position that we advertised!

Cindi simply checked the Facebooks of her children's friends in a very detailed fashion. Consequently, she found out things in one case that was very disturbing. I cannot go into great detail, but it involved cultic practices of one peer that would have put her daughter at great risk regarding safety.

The dinners were simply a way to get to know her children's friends better. In one instance, her son's friend revealed to the mom that his parents were split up and hardly ever at home. He then shared of his struggle with drugs that no one knew about.

The fun surveys are just that. It asks fun questions such as, if you could be a singer in any band, who would you be? What animal do you like best? What flavor of jelly beans do you like best? Then it throws in a few serious questions like, how often do you stay angry and how fast is fast to you on the highway?

The answers can be most revealing. I actually have modified the questions and now use this idea myself. The key to this story is that you never know what you will find unless you look. Many times, you simply find good in your peer evaluation. However, when you do find something harmful, it does validate your looking.

Regarding creativity, we use our creativity many times on the job and in the organizations that we are involved in unto proficiency and promotion. It is awesome when we use this same creativity regarding our children.

Story #7 – Ticks, Peanut Butter, & a Gun Cabinet

Dr. Joe is a professor at a very prestigious university. He is also a hunter, a gun collector, a dad, and a granddad. In all honesty, Dr. Joe is a tough guy and very opinionated! His wife has read the books that I have written and is a true advocate of safety. Accordingly, she shared the information that I have disseminated with her husband.

He was not impressed and even felt that my ideas on safety infringed on his individual rights. He especially did not like my emphasis on safety regarding ticks and making sure that his guns were in a cabinet or safe & securely locked. I believe in the 2nd amendment too but also believe in erring on the side of caution.

He stated that he never was bothered by a deer tick and never would be no matter what. His philosophy was basically, "just leave me alone." Interestingly enough, after Dr. Joe hunted with one of his grandchildren, this child who was 13 did come down with Lyme's Disease. Thankfully, the boy's mom diagnosed it quickly and its affects were minimal. This is not always the case.

This was an eye opener for Dr. Joe and to his credit (with the help of his wife!), he made a mindset change. He became more careful with his guns and became much more involved in safety issues, especially child safety. In fact, he became much more empathetic towards others in need. A powerful example of this was as follows.

One of his friends had a grandson who was 6-years-old who had a peanut allergy. Most people do not realize this but 1 in 13 children in America have some type of allergic reaction to peanuts. Prior to the incident with his grandson and the Lyme's Disease, by his own admission, he would have had a minimal reaction to the peanut allergy.

However, he found out about a possible solution for this boy that was validated by trail studies, now approved by the FDA. It sounds strange, but it is a peanut flour that when ingested creates an immunity to the allergy. It does not mean that the boy could now eat peanut butter. What it means is that if something like peanut butter is inadvertently eaten, it will not harm him as prior. I do not know how many children that this works for, but it did significantly help this little boy.

The main principle conveyed in this story is the following. Safety issues can many times be easily dismissed because they don't seem to apply to us due to our prior experiences. However, this does not mean that we should exempt ourselves from their reality. The truth is that we do have to deal with them. As we do, our children and the children of our neighbors and friends will be greatly benefited by us.

Story#8 – Power of Right Strategies

In both our parental attributes and wisdom keys sections, knowing your children was emphasized. Herein, I want to share Mr. & Mrs. Smith's story regarding their daughter Shelly. Shelly had been an excellent athlete since elementary school. She excelled in soccer, running, basketball, and softball.

When she was in 8th grade, she was doing really well on the middle school track team. About half-way through the season, she wanted to quit. Both her parents strongly encouraged her to stick it out. She did and excelled. In 9th grade, Shelly chose to run Cross-Country. She was doing well but half-way through the season was experiencing a lot of anxiety and wanted to quit.

However, just like in 8th grade, her parents strongly encouraged her to continue. However, this time, it did not seem to work. Shelly become anorexic and that's when the family came in for counseling. Anorexia is of course an eating disorder that affects many. During the counseling process, two things became apparent.

The first was that Shelly was somehow correlating running with a need to lose weight. The second was that her parents were not understanding her. They both ran competitively and simply thought that it was a phase that she would come out of. Very simply, they were wrong. For some reason, Shelly simply could not deal with running.

In many years of counseling, I have had several girls who were runners struggle with anorexia. Over half the time it doesn't work out. Shelly's parents had done everything they could to get her out of this stage. They even showed her a movie about running Icon, Steve Prefontaine. This went on for a few weeks.

Finally, I told them that they needed to change their strategy. This is what this whole story is about. There are times when your children are suffering due to a strategy that you are using that is simply wrong. When Shelly's parents completely, 100% accepted the reality that Shelly was not in a phase, but simply unable to deal with her situation, everything changed.

Her struggle with Anorexia, although it took some time was overcome. As well, her relationship with her parents improved. What was interesting is that Shelly wisely never ran again. However, she lettered 3 years in varsity Softball and loved it. Shelly very simply struggled with the individuality of running but prospered in a team-oriented sport. In the raising of your children, strategies are so significant. Different times, it is necessary to adapt as our children change.

<u>Story #9 – Understanding Triggers</u>

A trigger is something that usually elicits a negative response. Ryan's story starts in 2nd grade. He is like most 2nd graders. However, he is active and does his best when he has hands on activities. In first grade, he did well, in large part due to his teacher Mrs. Smith. Mrs. Smith was patient and was very affirming. As well, she created centers in the classroom that were conducive to Ryan's strengths.

Second grade was very different. In just the second week of school Ryan came home crying and angry. His teacher took away his recess time due to his getting out of his seat. She also told him not to be so hyper. His teacher contacted Ryan's parents. She suggested that he might need special intervention. She also shared that his attitude was inappropriate.

When talking on the phone, with the parents, I was so disturbed that I asked them to come to my office as soon as they could. They were concerned that Ryan was in need of special education due to his hyperactivity. They were concerned about Ryan's attitude. This was correlative to the teacher's phone call.

Having taught in the Public-School System for years, my take on the situation was very different. To me, it was not Ryan that was the problem. It was the teacher triggering him due to not understanding him and inaccurately labeling him. First of all, she had no right to call him hyper and label him as such.

The next day, I went with them to talk to the principal, He was very good with us. The parents were good people but did not understand fully the dynamics of triggers. To be quite honest, I made known to the principal in a strong way that this child should never have been labeled hyper. Her negativity triggered Ryan to the point that he began to hate school and feel bad about himself.

In this case, his teacher was reprimanded (this does not usually happen) and he was moved to another 2nd grade class. Ryan did extremely well and guess what? In the middle of 4th grade, he was identified as gifted and at the top of his class.

We need to identify both positive and negative triggers regarding our children. Then we need to accentuate the positive triggers and minimize the negative. I think to myself many times how many Ryan's are there who are misperceived due to their being seen through negative triggers rather than who they really are.

Janice came to the center with a friend. Janice was 18 at the time and her friend was 18 as well. They were both college freshman. Janice's friend was concerned because Janice had not attended classes and was not doing well. To make a long story short, Janice had received unwanted advances by an employee of the university. Janice was of strong moral character and rebuffed them.

She knew of another student who had this happen to her as well by the same individual. Consequently, she felt the need to contact appropriate authorities. This precious young lady was struggling so much due to a trigger that had never been dwelt with.

Janice had been sexually abused by a friend of the family at age 10. She shared of the incident readily, but it was not received as she had expected. She was told that she misinterpreted the persons actions. When she was not believed regarding her being abused, it devasted her. It caused her to isolate herself for a time. As well, it caused her to enter into a mindset of mistrust regarding disclosure.

Consequently, she associated disclosure with heartache and pain. Herein, we began to talk about this correlation. Accordingly, she began to see that the initial experience that triggered her mind to think that this situation would be no different was not the truth. We then discussed the specific variables that were involved in her current situation.

They included a dean that was very reputable, this happening to two other girls, and her being seen running to her room crying by another student after the man tried to grope her. This would validate her story.

You see, the key is to identify triggers in your children and then minimize and hopefully negate them. Kirsten became much more peaceful in our session.

Two days later, she shared with the dean (her friend went with her) and the incident was thoroughly investigated. It turned out that two other girls came forward making five altogether counting Kirsten and the man was dismissed.

It is important to note that once the trigger is identified, it is to be addressed as soon as possible. Many times, we put incidents of harm in the back of our mind, thinking that this takes care of the issue.

However, what is in the back of our mind when elicited by a similar situation will trigger us and can cause us to do something harmful to our self or others. Again, this is a key to parental responsibility. Our children need us to help them understand themselves. Our understanding of triggers enables us to bring this understanding to them. At different times, counseling can be of benefit as well.

Story #10 – Understanding Pressure & Dealing with it

Pressure comes to our children in many different ways. For our purposes regarding our children, pressure is defined as a need to do something even though the action has adverse consequences.

Interestingly enough, pressure can be elicited by both strengths and weaknesses. For example, if a 14-year-old girl or boy is seemingly mature beyond their years, they can gravitate towards relationships that they are not ready for. Pressure of course also comes via weaknesses as well. For example, if a young person at the age of 12 has a need for peer acceptance to the point of doing things that can be harmful to obtain it, they are very vulnerable.

This need for acceptance can be due to a myriad of reasons. They include rejection by significant others, lack of encouragement, or perceived personal failure.

Sometimes, it is simply a matter of a developmental struggle. It needs to be mentioned that being vulnerable to pressure to fit in does not necessarily mean that parents made a mistake to cause this need. However, it is critical that parents understand the reality of these needs in their child.

Sometimes, it is difficult for parents to comprehend the pressure on our children. From elementary school, social media can be a significant part of their lives.

From middle school, due to Facebook, Snapchat, and Twitter, everything is both accentuated and scrutinized. As well, social media is now the gauge of success for someone's self-worth. For example, the more likes an individual obtains, many times the more accepted he or she feels. This is why a number of our youth are taking the "Tide Pod Challenge", as shared prior.

This challenge involves literally ingesting Tide pods and then showing the reaction which can be deadly on social media. The number one reason that those participating in the challenge gave for doing it was to get more likes on Facebook.

Herein, I want to share with you Evan's story and the story of his parents. Evan is an only child and ever since he was in Kindergarten, he was involved with bikes. By the time, he was in 8th grade, he was doing well in motor-cross, skate boarding, and diving at the community park.

Evan was very nice, but never seemed to fit in with his peers at school. Possibly, this was due to his being smaller in stature than most of his class mates at this time. His not being accepted at school and being a risk taker definitely made him vulnerable to harm. Fortunately, his parents understood this reality. From 5th grade, they were very proactive regarding Evan's inclinations regarding risk taking.

They had a great relationship with him and utilized a number of wisdom keys that have been shared with you. This included role play, super analogies, and lots of communication. The following conveys how it really paid off.

In March of his 8th grade year, he was with some older boys. They were doing jumps on dirt bikes that they should not have been doing. The older boys then prodded Evan to do a very dangerous jump that he knew he should not do.

Here is the key. Even though he wanted to impress these older boys, he was equipped to handle the situation. With his parents, he had role played this type of scenario many times. He did exactly as he role played. He simply went his own way. Amidst being called various names, he resolutely went his own way.

In counseling, he also shared with me an analogy that his parents gave him years prior about never jumping off a cliff. This simple analogy stuck in his mind and was a true deterrent to him endangering himself.

Evan is now in 10th grade. He has grown up emotionally and had a growth spurt physically as well. He is still a little bit of a class clown but has a great group of friends. He is also very compassionate towards those who are struggling with their self-concept.

Story #11

Our last two stories are very recent. This one is in context of domestic safety. It conveys the power of words and the power of the mind. "Donald" when knowing that I was writing this book encouraged me to use his story.

I had been working with Donald for almost 8 months due to his struggle with alcohol. He is a good provider for his wife and two children, ages 8 and 10. However, he did have anger issues as well.

He had shared that his dad was very tough on him when growing up, being verbally abusive. As well, he at times was physically aggressive toward him. Donald travelled hours from out of state to come to the counseling center. We also conversed on the phone. To make a long story short, I asked him to view the movie, *I can Only Imagine.* The movie is a real-life account of an individual who experienced domestic abuse at the hands of his father.

The movie had a tremendous impact on him in two ways. First, it gave him a greater hope than he had ever had before regarding himself. Very simply it has accelerated his own wholeness and he is doing better than ever before. Second, it caused him to see as never before the harm that his negativity and hurtful words had on his two sons.

Donald was very distraught as he became aware of his hurtfulness. Accordingly, I shared with him the three R's. They include repentance, re-speaking, and re-affirming.

Repentance is defined by the *Meriam-Webster Dictionary* as having regret to the point that you will change for the good. Re-Speaking, entails speaking again, but in a manner that negates words of negativity and harm. Re-Affirming involves entering into a place of consistent encouragement. It is creating an environment of peace and safety. The key to all of these variables is consistency.

There has to be a commitment to speak positively and affirm over and over again. Thankfully, this simple paradigm is bearing fruit with his children. This story conveys the power of words, both positive and negative. It also shows the power of the visual modality. Again, what we hear and see, especially from a parent is extremely influential.

Words can produce life or profound pain. As parents, we need to speak words of life. However, thankfully, if we make a decision to change our speaking as necessary, it can undo much heart ache and pain.

Story #12 – Perseverance and Unconditional Love

Our last story revolves around Dory. She is now 15 and has been through a lot. She has been in and out of the foster care system since she was six years old. Some of the experiences were positive, but others were very detrimental. By the time she was 13, she was both very angry and rebellious.

It was at this time, that she was put into another foster home. The foster parents were well aware of her profile and had met with Dory prior to their commitment. They actually called me prior to their consent.

I will never forget the following comment. They shared that they felt that they saw something very positive in her. There were some tough times, especially for the first 3 months. This is when I became involved. Herein, the *Through His Eyes* program was instituted. This program is used in the context of helping someone who has been harmed, enter into wholeness and learn how to overcome.

For the next 3 months, Dory started to show signs of trust. Her foster parents then made a commitment to adopt her (if it would be approved). It seemed to backfire as she was very disruptive in school the very next day. This is not unusual for two reasons. The first is due to children like this having a difficult time believing that they really can be loved unconditionally. Therefore, there is an adverse reaction. The second is to do something bad to see if the love is really real.

In Dory's case, I think that it was the former. The parents and I met with her after the school suspension. She knew why she did what she did. We laughed, and we cried. It was the beginning of great things for Dory. I am crying now as I share her story.

I purposely saved this story for last for two reasons. First, there is no substitute for unconditional love. It causes a parent to endure in hard times, seeing strength in their child even when they are struggling.

This perceived strength by the parent is picked up by your child. It then translates into them entering into like perception. Second, it shows the reality of change. Dory's parents perceived potential in her. Through love and perseverance, the potential within Dory became realized. It continues to be realized in an amazing way.

In a recent session, she began to cry. I thought that something was wrong. However, there was nothing wrong, her crying was in response to a song that she shared with me. It is called *Reckless Love*, sung by Cory Asbury. It is a song of hope revolving around a love that is unconditional. I had never heard of the song, but it turns out that many now have.

It has now received over 15 million hits on social media! Why has this song taken off like it has? I believe it is because our children relate most to hope and love. Regarding Dory, I want to share something that she conveyed that I feel is significant. She shared that when she was struggling, she was extremely angry. She was angry due to being hurt and not having hope. Due to this mindset, she gravitated towards listening to music that fueled her anger. She had thoughts of harming people and places, even herself. Now, she is listening to songs of life and relating to them.

Thankfully, although she was going down a road of destruction, she did not continue to do so. She is now going down a road that is amazing. This is because she is safe, surrounded by unconditional love.

The most difficult thing about this chapter is that there are so many more stories that could have been shared. Again, each story has emphasized a variable correlative to one of our wisdom keys.

This was done to encourage you, to accentuate the fruitfulness that comes from them as they are acted out. It is not always easy to do so, but it is always a privilege and responsibility in regards to parenting. The exciting thing is that we can make our own stories, stories of love and fulfillment.

Chapter 6

Increasing the Odds

Many precious people due to having experienced harm in some way, have a degree of unsurety when it comes to safety.

Bound to Happen

There are truly more and more incidents of harm in today's society. From home invasions to abuse to shootings, many are being affected.

As well, due to social media of today, these incidents are conveyed over and over again. Consequently, many people feel that harm will inevitably come their way. They certainly hope not but feel that it is inevitable due to its prevalence. Herein, there simply is not much that can be done about it.

Whatever Happens Just Happens

From talking to many people over the years, there is also a mindset of "whatever happens just happens". This mindset is very prevalent.

In this context, the variable of being lucky or unlucky is often referred to.

Prepared for Harm

Different individuals emphasize preparing for harm as opposed to proactively emphasizing safety. The rationale for this mindset revolves around the prevalence of harm.

All of these mindsets are understandable due to the prevalence of harm.

Prescription

However, one of the primary keys to safety is being ahead of the curve. It is entering into a proactive mindset as shared. Many feel that safety is more random than prescribed. Things just happen, whatever will be, will be.

Mario Smithton, a professor that I came to know had this mindset, I did not utilize his story in our last chapter. I wanted to save it until now.

Mario is a brilliant man. However, he had a definite fear regarding safety issues. They included both domestic and sexual abuse. This was due to what he experienced and saw. He pointed out to me that you cannot predict 100% of the time what will take place. I shared that I agreed with him but countered by sharing the following. It is not about being able to predict perfectly, 100% of the time. It is about probability.

For example, one cannot say that their child will never fall off their bike. However, with safety training regarding riding and wearing a helmet, this will significantly increase the probability of a child never being significantly hurt while riding.

In the context of increasing the probability of safety regarding both domestic and sexual abuse, I listed a number of variables and strategies. I then shared the correlation between the degree of proactive measures taken in those areas and the probability of safety occurring.

He expressed his surprise at the number of measures that were available regarding these areas. So many people simply do not realize the provisions available in the area of safety. Many times, this is due to simply never being informed of these provisions. As well, with those like Dr. Smithton, experiences of harm can be so emotionally devastating that one never considers there even being a provision.

Dr. Smithton actually cried after our conversation. Instead of choosing to be bitter, he chose to be better. He is now using his talents to work where individuals and families who are vulnerable to harm regarding abuse.

Readiness

One cannot underestimate the power of readiness. The majority of our wisdom keys have revolved around this variable. It is so powerful because it causes you as a parent to have leverage in your quest for safety.

When I think of readiness, I think of those who were ready and those who were not. The following is a simple example that illustrates this point. Two friends in the same youth group signed up for a weekend ski trip. Both were not at all adept at skiing.

Accordingly, both sets of parents talked to the boys. One set of parents assertively talked to their son. He got the message and promised to only go down the beginner's slope. He was ready to do right. Unfortunately, regarding the other boy, his dad made light of his inexperience and told him to do what he felt he could do.

Herein, he was not ready to act cautiously. This is because a decision was not made prior to the trip. Consequently, when this young man's peers were egging him on not to just to go down the "baby" slope, he caved in. He hurt his leg, but thankfully not severely.

However, it could have been much more damaging. The key between the two boys was readiness. One made a decision prior to the event. The other did not, being indecisive.

All Areas

The need to be ready is necessary in all areas of safety. The following are just four examples of many areas.

Driving

It is obvious that state requirements throughout the country regarding obtaining a driver's license have increased. More hours of drive time prior to taking the test are required. As well, in different states, the age limit has increased. This will translate into less accidents and less fatalities.

However, even with the new requirements, one cannot assume that just because your child passes their drivers test, that they do not yet need to work on weak areas.

For example, if you as a parent know that your child is still not confident on the interstate, you need to address this issue with them. You cannot just assume or hope that they will not be hurt.

Herein, it is necessary to work with them. This is necessary, even if your child insists that you don't! As well, it is imperative that we teach our children to drive defensively. This again, is in the context of readiness.

We need to daily make driving safety a priority. However, it is significant to note that there are more teenage fatalities from driving between Memorial Day and Labor Day than any other time of the year.

D.U.I. Visuals

In the area of driving under the influence, authorities are using creative visuals to dissuade drinking and driving. Statistics show that it is helping in this area.

Again, this is an example of being proactive. It does make a difference when we do not sit back and just accept harm. When we fight against the problem, there is a direct effect that is positive.

Equipment and Fields

Regarding being proactive, the evolution of athletic equipment speaks for itself. From football, baseball, and bicycle helmets to new practice protocols, safety is at the forefront. At the same time, there is always a need for daily awareness.

At a little league baseball game, an 8-year-old was hit in the head by another boy warming up in the on-deck circle. There simply was not enough room as there should have been to walk by.

Thankfully, the boy hurt recovered. Changes were made to the field. However, it never should have happened.

Herein, I am a strong advocate of either having an individual or committee regarding safety relative to any event.

Years ago, while teaching high school, in the summer, I helped supervise a softball league. I cancelled a game due to wet conditions. Many did not like the decision, but I knew that playing would compromise the safety of the players.

While coaching track at the high school level, I had an assistant coach who ran the middle school program.

I attended a middle school meet and could not believe what I saw. Two of the boys and three of the girls running the hurdles fell. After the meet, I asked the coach how much practice time these young athletes had regarding the hurdles. He replied, very little.

I told him that he put these athletes in jeopardy regarding their safety. I also told him that he would be dismissed if this ever happened again.

I assumed that this coach would know better. However, we cannot assume. We need to appoint specific people to oversee safety and educate them.

Courthouse Safety

Just a few weeks ago, I was attending a trial at a courthouse in a county in Northwest Pennsylvania. I was amazed to find that there were no metal detectors as I entered. I just walked upstairs to the courtroom. In this courthouse, murder cases, high profile drug cases, and hotly contested domestic disputes take place.

As I was walking out, a retired police officer asked this, "are they waiting for someone to be killed before they do what is necessary?" I replied, I truly hope not.

I personally believe that all court houses should be required to have metal detectors at a minimum. We should never have to wait for a disaster to be motivated to do what is simply commonsensical.

Truly through desire and wisdom, we can increase the odds of our children being safe. This is to be our mission.

Chapter 7

Predictive Analytics

Carnegie Mellon University in Pittsburgh is one of the premier research institutes in the world. The university receives millions of dollars in grants annually for research in various areas.

Recently, I became aware of a program that the university was involved in through an article in the Pittsburgh Post-Gazette newspaper.

It involved a program that was devised to reduce the number of fires related to abandoned buildings in urban areas.

These fires of course posed a great safety risk to both people and the buildings nearby. There are hundreds of these buildings standing.

This is due to the lack of money available to demolish them in accordance with environmental regulations.

Due to this reality, those making an effort to offer a solution to this problem asked two questions.

What if we could find a way to determine which houses posed the greatest immediate risk? What could be done to reduce the risk?

In this context, it was decided to utilize predictive analytics as a way to answer these questions.

Predictive analytics involves identifying data that when complied and analyzed can convey the probability of something occurring.

Herein, it was especially applicable to identifying the most problematic buildings regarding potential fires. However, it is applicable to virtually all areas of safety.

Regarding the buildings specific to the project mentioned, utilizing the predictive analytics paradigm, definite success was realized.

Buildings were addressed in a quick but quality manner. Different variables were used in this assessment e.g. electrical make-up, age, location, type of structure.

Then, a prediction regarding the potential of that structure being problematic regarding fire was made.

It was then submitted to appropriate authorities. Then, when accepted those ascertained to have the highest probability of being a fire hazard were torn down (as funds were available).

The result was that less fires developed making the communities affected were safer.

I have shared the concept of predictive analytics for two main reasons.

The first is to reinforce this reality that the majority of time, things simply do not happen. There are variables that contribute to that which does happen.

The second reason is so that you can use this concept in your own life regarding safety.

In fact, this concept is the key to what is being presented in this manuscript.

Again, the concept of predictive analytics is in the context of probability.

If-Then

Probability can be easily seen in the If-Then equation. If you do this (something positive), then (something positive) will occur.

Let me share a few examples regarding the If-Then equation. The first is somewhat humorous.

I am sharing this purposely because the area of safety can be very sobering in different respects. As a result, I think that it is important to share different things in a relaxed manner.

This example revolves around a little league team (8 and 9-year-old kids). This is an age when there is a transition from coach pitch to the little leaguers pitching themselves.

A friend of mine asked me to go to a game to watch his son play who was a very good athlete.

At the game, one of the little league pitchers was not very accurate. In fact, he hit five different batters. Thankfully, his velocity was not very high, so there was no significant injury. After the game, I talked to the dad who also was a coach. He shared that they had to face this young pitcher next week!

I simply shared that the chance of him hitting batters again was very high. I then suggested that in practice, his team should practice ducking and side-stepping pitches, so they don't get hit. He took my suggestion and they did! It actually helped in the next game against this pitcher.

Sometimes it is not hard to predict what will happen, if certain variables are in place. Likewise, it is then easier to find solutions to what one will face.

Everything written in this book is to increase the probability of you and your family being safe.

Utilizing the babysitting form and the sleepover checklist increases the probability of you and your child being safe.

Peer evaluation regarding your children's relationships will increase the probability of them being safe from wrong influences.

Again, probability is the key to safety and success. In reality, it is the key to virtually anything we do.

This is true in the area of cancer treatment. As a counselor, I am involved with a number of individuals who have and are battling cancer.

In my experience in this area, it seemed like different hospitals had a higher success rate than others.

I shared this with a sister of a man that I was visiting who had cancer. She happened to be an advocate for cancer patients who did not have anyone.

She then shared with me that hospitals are rated in different areas of care. She then showed me on the computer those that were four star versus those that were two star.

I was very surprised as I never heard of such a system. She then shared of the variables intrinsic to the rating.

In this context, she shared of a friend who was receiving treatment for cancer at a hospital that was rated low. She shared that the treatment being used was seen as outdated by many. He was not doing well. With her advice, her friend switched hospitals, received different treatment with very good results.

Obtaining treatment at a higher rated medical facility does not guarantee success. However, in such a serious situation, wisdom entails doing everything that you can do to give yourself the best chance to succeed.

This scenario regarding cancer has been life changing in my interaction with those fighting the greatest battle of their lives.

This exemplifies what predictive analytics is all about and the significance of this principle.

Due to its influence of everyday life, I want to share 12 more examples of how you can integrate this principle into your everyday life regarding safety.

Practice and Proficiency

This is a simple but very powerful example of predictive analytics.

The more you practice something, the more you work on something, the more proficient and successful you will be.

This is easily seen in athletics. For example, the more you practice shooting in basketball, the better scorer you will be.

Michael Jordan, who many say is the greatest basketball player of all time was always good. However, coming out of college at North Carolina, his three-point shot was not strong.

What did he do? He shot thousands of three-point shots in practice. These practice shots turned into him shooting proficiently from three-point range.

This principle is easily seen in education. The more a student practices math problems, the more proficient he will become.

Regarding college boards, MCAT or LSAT tests, the more you do practice tests, the better you will do on the real tests. We see this principle in finding solutions to issues. The more we are proactive in trying to find solutions, the more proficient we will be in finding solutions.

The great thing about this reality is that success breeds the desire to practice more and work harder.

When I taught high school, I coached a cross-country running team. We started a 300-mile running club and went undefeated. Within 5 years, we were up to 700 miles per summer and won 50 meets in a row. We simply ran more miles than any other school. It works! However, if we do not practice, the probability of failure is likely as well.

Education Yields Results

Ignorance is not bliss. Where abuse, bullying and Opioids prevail, may times these areas have not been targeted educationally.

Information is power. Information coupled with motivation and wisdom brings freedom. True education is multi-faceted and consistent in being put before our children.

In your family, it should always be put before your children. It brings forth understanding and abhorrence for wrong doing.

In a school, what we desire is in our mission statement. It is incorporated into our assemblies and in our policies.

To the degree that our children are educated on issues is the degree that they will do right and their safety will be ensured.

The Power of Modeling

There is definitely a need for role models in our society as never before. This modeling must start in the family.

The greatest predictor of whether a son will grow up and respect and honor his wife is how he sees his dad treat his mom. It is equally true regarding how a young woman will grow up and treat her husband.

Again, things do not just happen. There is a direct correlation between parental behavior and the behavior of your children.

You do not need a crystal ball to look into the future. You only need to look at yourself to see what will occur.

Your future and the future of your children is to a definite degree predictable. This is good news due to our ability and desire to do right.

Set Times

In our busy lives, it is increasingly harder to find time to spend together with our children. Herein, it is critical that we see making time not as a possibility but a decision. Very simply, you and I will never find time, we have to make time.

I want to reinforce the concept of set times. A set time is simply when you set up a consistent predetermined time to get together with your child or children to accomplish a specific objective. The following are a few examples of set times.

Game Night

This of course has to be age appropriate. For example, for your 7 to 9 years old, you might play Uno or Monopoly every Saturday night from 7:00-8:15pm. It is simple, but statistics strongly show that a simple game night realizes both family bonding and emotional strength.

However, the key is establishing set times, a schedule when chores are to be done.

Study Time

Set times regarding your children's school work will help them significantly. Whether your child is in first grade, sixth grade or ninth grade, established study times will be of benefit both to your children and to you.

Set study times benefit your children because it negates distractions and instills discipline regarding you trying to get them to study.

I'll study after I watch this program. I'll study after I talk to my friend. I'll study sometime, don't bother me. Sound familiar? The earlier you start utilizing set times with your children, the easier it will be. I recommend starting in first grade.

The greatest thing is that your children will come to see this as a positive. As well, when those utilizing set study times are compared to random study times, academic achievement is over all higher by those utilizing set times.

Chore Times

The same is true when set times are used regarding chores, it takes away all the drama. Chores of course should not be excessive but reasonable responsibilities that are age appropriate.

As with studying, getting children to do their chores has become a battleground for many parents. If a child is given chores that are palatable and reinforced with verbal praise and a possible allowance, it can certainly cause chores to be seen in a positive light.

Sharing Times

A sharing time is when a parent or parents simply communicate with their child in a prescribed or open-ended fashion. Again, it is a set time. It might be a breakfast with mom or dad on Saturday or a time on Wednesday night just to ask how things are going.

You may be surprised how much this enhances your relationship with your child and how much he or she looks forward to it. It will also generalize to your child opening up to you in times of need.

<u>Creativity</u>

I have given you different areas where set times can easily be utilized. However, I encourage you to use your creativity to explore other areas.

One parent shared with me that she has one hour set times called, "Blackout". It is when her three teen-age children cannot use their cellphones, watch television or use any other electronic device.

They can read a book, write a letter, do a physical activity or even talk to each other. This parent said that it is her favorite time of the day!

It is a time that really benefits her children as it enables them to function without external stimuli.

The key is set times. When you proactively introduce and follow through on set times with your children, you are helping them in a tremendous way.

In today's society, all around your children is unsurity! Will the student beside me on the bus try to bully me? Will my friend think I am weird because I do not want to go to the party on Saturday?

In an environment of unsurity, our children need structure. They need set times. Your children are just not going to gravitate towards doing chores or studying at the same time each day or will put down their cellphones for a time just because they know that this is good for them!

Accordingly, as parents it is so important for us to be intentional. We need to do what is necessary to give our children the greatest chance possible to succeed. The utilization of set times is definitely something that can increase the probability of their success.

Sleep and Breakfast

Studies show emphatically that children – young and older could benefit from more sleep. Herein, in the context of our last variable of set times, it is important to set a time that your children go to sleep.

The amount of sleep a child gets directly effects both his emotional strength and academic performance.

I have put sleep and breakfast together due to their strong effect on our children. As parents, we need to provide nutritious meals for our children. In the context of predictive analytics, nutrition, and strength go together.

Your children from a young age will go to bed when you set a time for them and eat what you put before them. Again, they will gravitate naturally in our society towards staying up too late and wanting to eat chips, pop, and ice cream more than whole grains and vegetables.

We need to do what is in their best interests to give them the best chance to prosper.

Mental Health-Bullying

In regard to predictive analytics, utilizing goals, and objectives almost always guarantees greater success regarding safety issues.

This particular goal works with a small or large family unit. The goal is to only use positive words and not negative words.

Positive words are that which lift up and encourage. Negative words are that which discourage and degrade.

Parents and children set a goal of using their words in a positive manner, not only applies to your child and your children, but of course to the parents as well.

In this goal relating to positive words, one does not count the positive words or negative words, keeping score.

However, when inappropriate words are spoken it is recognized as wrong. As well, when positive words are shared. They are reinforced. Then, for accountability purposes, weekly sharing as a family of how things went regarding the goal is recommended.

This simple goal does much more than many may think. It really does work! So many families struggle with being positive towards one another. From parent to parent, sibling relationships, and parent child relationship, this is an area of difficulty.

All too often, this area is not addressed in an objective fashion. Most of all families want positive interaction within their family. However, it is not enough to desire it. It has to be communicated from the parents in an open goal-oriented fashion. It then needs to be affirmed according to the priority that it really is.

Exercise and Diet

This is a sensitive subject but one that needs to be addressed. Like it or not, obesity is a real problem in the United States. For example, among those between the ages of 17-24, one in three Americans are considered obese.

In the military Occupational Physical Assessment Test (OPAT), a requirement to be able to enter military service, so many are unable to pass this test. The key is to start at an early age and make things fun.

Regarding diet, it is up to you as a parent to set the menu! This is best done from an early age. Children acquire taste for different things.

If you limit sugar (pies, cakes, candy, cookies, ice cream, pop), trans fats and processed foods in a commonsensical way, your child will benefit.

You of course need to replace the above with proteins, vegetables, fruits, and good cooking oils like Coconut, Extra Virgin oil, and Canola. It is simple, but it does take a little extra work. However, the results are very predictable and very good.

Regarding exercise, the key is starting and making it fun. As well, exercise needs to be individualized to your child's strengths and interests.

One child might enjoy running and another swimming. Other activities can include hiking, riding a bike, walking, tennis, soccer, and the list goes on and on!

The key is emphasizing the importance of exercise and correlating it with enjoyment.

Again, diet and exercise do not just magically appear in a child's mindset or lifestyle. It is that which is realized by prescription.

Vehicle Safety

Vehicle safety is a key in every family. Goals and objectives can certainly contribute to the probability of safety in this area. I recommend involving your children in vehicle safety from a young age. This may seem difficult to do but it is really not.

Herein, I want to share with you how to integrate your children in the goal setting process. As well, it is important for the parents to take the lead.

Regarding little children e.g. 3 to 6 years old, parents need to relate to where their children are at.

Accordingly, objectives such as never riding their bikes in the driveway without mommy or daddy being there and never going near the road are easily understood. As well, they need to know that they are never permitted to go into mommy or daddy's car without them. Also, that they can never unlock their seatbelt.

When children are older (7 to 14), safety regarding bicycles, four-wheelers and general protocol regarding driving is incorporated into goal setting.

This is where parental agreement is very significant. Parents need to agree on driving protocol. In a 65 MPH speed limit, what speed will you agree on? Will you be faithful to never pass when you should not? Will you establish zero tolerance regarding any type of road rage personally? How will you ride your four-wheeler?

I guarantee you that overall your children will drive very much like you do. Consequently, the objectives that you set, you have to abide your yourself.

Regarding a 5-year old, I had an interesting experience regarding vehicle safety. His parents shared it with me prior to a board meeting that I was at.

Two parents had agreed to not go over the speed limit near their housing complex. They explained to their little girl that this was to protect little children her age from being in an accident. Unfortunately, they were in a hurry and were 10 miles over the limit. The little girl abruptly, seeing the high speed confronted the parents! It was a wake-up call to them.

The little girl's awareness was realized due to goal setting and making her part of the process.

Regarding older children (15 to 19), the objectives continue to evolve. However, when you have started earlier, it does make it easier. Again, parental agreement and child involvement in goal setting is key.

Addressing the issue of vehicle safety in a proactive manner does make a tremendous difference. It truly does increase the probability of your children being safe.

Vehicle Selection and Confidence

I want to share one more aspect of vehicular safety relating to predictive analytics. This is due to the tremendous significance of this area of safety.

Two main variables will be focused upon. They include vehicle selection and the confidence level of driving different vehicles.

Regarding vehicle selection for your child, it is extremely important to be very selective.

As parents, we cannot just buy a car off the lot due to price or because our child likes a certain color.

I have shared this prior but want to accentuate the need to consider the impact that the type of car that you choose to let your child drive has on him or her. There is no doubt that if you choose or let your child drive a faster looking type car, there is a higher risk of being expected to go faster by peers.

A while ago, while on my local school board, I talked to a few state troopers involved in an accident prevention program.

They openly shared how they were surprised at the vehicles that parents let their children drive. Again, if you let your daughter or son drive a bright red, race car-type vehicle your putting them in greater jeopardy than if they drive a more conservative looking vehicle.

As well, SUV's are becoming increasingly popular due to their passenger capacity, teenagers just want to pile in after practice. It is difficult for the driver to say no. This obviously puts the driver and passengers at risk due to the correlation between the number of passengers in a vehicle and the chance of an accident.

Your young driver is still young! He or she is still establishing their identity. This is why it is imperative that we as parents address this issue.

We can do this by simple communication. First, we need to make sure that we do not assume that we know what their confidence level is. The need to have the freedom to honestly share that which they feel.

Second, they need to know that they will not be perceived as weak because of their lack of confidence regarding a certain vehicle.

This does not just apply to cars and trucks, but to ATV's and motorcycles as well.

Years ago, when I first started teaching, a lot of my neighbors rode dirt bikes, motorcycles, that were used off road. I went with them one Saturday but was not fully comfortable with riding with them.

However, I didn't say anything and rode. About half way up a large hill, I lost control and went down the hill with the motorcycle on top of me. I was bruised but thankfully not severely.

It really is important to ascertain our children's level of confidence regarding different vehicles. One simple way is simply to ask them. You can help them convey their confidence level by asking them, on a scale of 1 to 10 which 10 being the highest, share the number that best describes your confidence level. This simple gauge can convey much.

If it is low on one vehicle and high on another, then do one of two things. Have your child drive the car that they are most confident with or work with them until their confidence level rises regarding the other.

In the context of predictability, doing this will make them much safer.

Parental Confidence Level

The following variable brings balance to driver confidence regarding your child. This balance is you! You determine your child's confidence level through their input. As well, you determine their ability level to drive safely due to your observation.

Your child may think that they are ready to drive a motorcycle or ATV, but you know that they are not ready. Consequently, you have to be the deciding factor.

I do my best not to share negative scenarios, but I feel that the following needs to be shared. This is due to the importance of both vehicular safety and the importance of predictive analytics.

Decades ago, a young 18-year-old who was a real risk taker and his parents were in conflict. The 18-year-old son was going to go to college out west. He wanted his parents to buy him a new Jeep to use at school.

The parents could afford it but told him no. However, they said that they would purchase a regular car for him. This was because they knew that a Jeep (especially in the 1990's) was a high-risk vehicle for their son. However, unfortunately the parents gave in to their son's request. Regrettably, he lost control of the jeep while going at a high rate of speed and lost his life. I weep as I share this.

However, the results were predictable. As parents, we need to utilize predictability so tragedy is avoided.

Blue Light

In our 11th example of predictive analytics, I want to deal with a creative idea regarding those struggling with Heroin addiction.

It is of course best to be proactive in the prevention of opioid addiction. This has been addressed prior in the context of the wisdom keys that were shared. However, the following idea has saved lives regarding those currently fighting addiction.

Unfortunately, many Heroin addicts utilize fast food chain restrooms and other place of business to shoot up.

Consequently, business owners use blue light in the restrooms, so addicts cannot have adequate light to be able to shoot up. It is unfortunate that this need even exists, but it has actually helped cut down on the number of overdose deaths in many communities.

Very simply, people were hunting for any way possible to cut down overdose deaths. With the concept of the blue light came a prediction that lives would be saved. This prediction was realized in a strong way due to its ability to be duplicated.

Herein, I want to encourage you as a parent to utilize your creative abilities to bring about novel ideas that will bring about a greater degree of safety in all areas of life.

Predictive analytics should be the foundation of all areas of safety. It is based on simple logic and easily integrated into everyday life. Virtually everything in this text is based upon it.

Our goal as parents is certainly to do all that we can to ensure our children's safety. As times change, new challenges will arise. However, with these challenges, solutions will be realized as well. The key is to proactively pursue these solutions.

Grants and Scholarships

I want to close this chapter with an example that millions of parents can relate to. It involves you obtaining financial aid for your children's higher education experience.

You might say "what does predictive analytics have to do with obtaining money for your student's higher education costs?" I would answer much!

This is due to the following. The more proactive that parents are in looking for grants and scholarships to fund their children's higher education, the greater the chance that funding will be found.

Let me give you a recent example that conveys this reality. "Joe" and "Jill" have been concerned about paying for their daughter's college education since their daughter, Sarah was in middle school (8th grade).

They saved a modest sum of money each month, putting it into a special account. They also, in a non-pressuresome way encouraged their daughter to do her best academically knowing her grades could make her eligible for financial grants.

A year prior to Sarah graduating high school, everything escalated. This is because Sarah received early acceptance at a private college that coast about 72,000 dollars a year. That is a lot of money over 4 years!

During that year, Joe and Jill heard that possible assistance was available but that they had to invest quality time to procure what was available.

They both had full-time jobs but made a commitment to spend 3 hours Saturday morning together focusing on searching for scholarships and grants. As well, Jill would put in even more time following up leads that had been discovered.

They had some days where it seemed that there was not what they had thought. However, they continued and just prior to Sarah attending school, all 72,000 dollars was taken care of, debt free.

There is certainly a commitment that is necessary to bring about what these parents did. However, they were convinced that if they spent the time, then it would produce monetarily regarding their daughter's education.

It needs to be conveyed again that there will be challenges with any endeavor. Jill shared that with one grant application, she had to modify it and send it back six different times. However, it was worth it.

In conclusion, almost everyone would like to know the future. Almost everyone, would like to at least know how to have a better future. Predictive analytics gives you and I the ability to best effect our future. This is especially true in the context of safety.

Anytime that you, as a parent can increase the chance of your child being safe, you of course will want to do it. As well, the more convinced that you are of the increased probability of safety, the more positive you can be. In today's society, the ability to be positive and hopeful certainly goes a long way.

Chapter 8

≈⟊≈

You!

In our prior chapter, readiness and intentionality were emphasized. We saw that safety is obtainable! This is good news but does cause us as parents to have to come to the table, to face the challenges of today regarding our children. The following are variables and challenges that are necessary to be aware of and entered into.

Responsibility

When a child is born, they are profoundly vulnerable. They are in complete need of their parents as care givers to give them what they need in virtually every area of life. This dependence continues throughout the majority of the developmental stages of their lives.

<u>Physically</u>

A baby or young child (toddler) is not responsible for his nutritional and safety needs being met. You are of course the key. Your child will eat what is given him. He is not aware whether there are high led levels in the paint you use for his room. His or her physical viability is primarily dependent on you.

Now, as with each of the areas that will be discussed, the key is not providing, but the extent that you are providing. From proper diet and housing to clothing and environment, it is the parents' responsibility to realize quality provision. From birth to college, children do not just naturally grow intellectually. It is all about cultivation.

It is the parents' responsibility to provide interaction unto cultivating the intellectual potential within their child. Much of this cultivation takes place from birth to six years of age. Years ago, I came in contact with a woman who was struggling emotionally while raising her two younger children.

She provided little intellectual stimulation for the first years of their lives. Unfortunately, these precious boys are intellectually lacking to this day. The above reality exemplifies the principle of cultivation. As with safety in general, things do not just happen.

Through providing intellectual stimulus and interaction, parents can affect their children in a beneficial way. The greater the interaction, the greater the results. This includes a love for learning itself.

<u>Emotional</u>

Emotional strength and stability is another trait in our children that is affected by parental interaction. It is the responsibility of parents to provide an environment that promotes emotional strength.

This environment is to include consistent affirmation, appropriate discipline, and emotional expression.

From birth to adult hood, children are very vulnerable to their parents in the emotional realm. This is due to the innate emotional make up of a child. This vulnerability includes the need for positive emotional expression and no inappropriate verbal expression or harmful discipline.

The first involves the omission of emotional expression. This omission can be due to parents not paying attention to their children due to their own struggles such as alcohol or drug addiction. As well, there are certainly parents who love their children but get so busy that they lose track of the time needed to spend with their children.

There are also those who struggle in expressing positive emotions to their children due to personality weakness or negative experiences themselves. Regarding hurtful words and actions such as wrongful discipline e.g. prolonged timeout. Parents have a responsibility to protect the emotions of their children.

Even as it is necessary to protect our children physically, it is equally necessary to protect our children emotionally. As well, we need to strengthen our children emotionally. This is done in part by interacting in a positive emotional way with our children.

Social

It is imperative that we teach our children to be socially responsible as well. This includes respect for others, moral attributes such as honesty and kindness, as well as helping others. What parents reinforce will be seen as appropriate and good. What parents do not reinforce will be seen as inappropriate and wrong.

It is a responsibility to reinforce what is right. It is also a privilege. Again, the key to parental responsibility is you. Your children's physical, intellectual, emotional, and social well-being is profoundly dependent on you.

Work

The variable of work is not always emphasized in parenting. However, it should be! There will be a commitment required to realize anything that is worthwhile in life. This is especially true regarding our children. From getting up in the middle of the night to hold a crying baby to waiting up in the late-night hour due to your son or daughter being late it involves commitment.

I have received many letters of encouragement regarding our promotion of child safety. However, different people have conveyed that they think that I am asking too much of them regarding keeping their children safe and especially regarding time that they should spend with their child interacting.

I understand that we are all busy trying to provide for our families. I also understand that time is at a premium. However, I also understand that there is no substitute for you! Parenting requires much, and it is inconvenient at times. However, that which is of the greatest benefit does require the greatest commitment our children are of supreme benefit.

Accountability

Accountability is of tremendous importance regarding every area of life. It is especially important in the area of parenting and safety. If you would walk into an insurance agent office to obtain car insurance, you would undoubtedly be asked how many accidents you were involved in (if any) in the past two years.

What do you think would happen if you smiled and said, "Just seven accidents in the last two years, but I am improving. It was four two years ago and only three this year." The agent would obviously send you packing. In this area, you have to know what an appropriate driving record is. You have to know how to be a driver commensurate with that which is appropriate. You have to commit to the process accordingly.

I know that the answer of seven accidents is certainly out of the norm for two years. It seems almost unbelievable. However, in the area of parenting, I have asked a parent. In the last two years, how many times have you screamed at your child, actually calling him names that would be deemed as hurtful? I have had various parents glibly say, perhaps 10 or 12 times. Unfortunately, you cannot take away their insurance, but you have to make it an issue of focus.

The reason that things like this (even among parents who do love their children) can happen is usually due to a lack of accountability. In parenting, we need to have appropriate objectives and a reasonable way of measuring them. This is in the context of personal weaknesses and strengths. As well, it is in the context of our interaction with our children.

True accountability should involve individuals that understand your objectives. They also should be those that you can trust and preferably people that can promote the fulfillment of these objectives. They can include spouse to spouse accountability, those whom you are friends with, or those that you respect who have fulfilled these objectives with their own children.

Again, the key variable is you. You can dismiss this variable of accountability or embrace it. At the very least, you should enter into both self-accountability and spousal accountability as well.

Accountability is a safeguard for all of us. It is amazing how we can be unaware of habits being formed.

A friend of mine who is a doctor and his wife said they had no idea of how much money they were spending on eating out, until they added it up. They then set a budget to help in this area. Accountability is a safeguard, but it is also a vehicle of growth. It acts as a motivational force as we gain wisdom from others and see results.

Role Model

We have addressed this variable in prior chapters. I simply want to reiterate that you are the primary role model in the life of your children. They may have a poster of a singer or athlete on the wall of their room. However, in their heart, you have precedence relationally and in the context of their identity. There is simply no one that has the ability to influence them as much as you do as a parent. This includes both your words and your actions.

You have probably heard the expression, "a picture is worth a thousand words." When your child sees you watching an off-color video or abusing alcohol, it will stick. There is a principle in counseling that I want to share at this time. I refer to it as mental or emotional imprinting. Imprinting occurs when through words or actions, what is said or done becomes a part of your mind or emotions.

It can be unto great benefit or great harm. All of us can remember incidents that still seem fresh in our minds, whether good or bad. I can remember when my mom was in the hospital and not expected to live. She had just been given the sacrament of last rights. (She did survive the battle). On the way to the hospital, my dad wept and turned to me saying, "son, you are all I have now." It is something I never forgot.

At the same time, experiences of pain can affect us equally in an adverse manner. It is amazing to me that when a child is physically hurt or verbally abused by a parent, he or she will replicate this behavior. It is not because they want to. It is because they have been imprinted with it. This does not mean that they cannot overcome it. It is not an excuse, but the imprinting is real.

I know that this is strong stuff, and this is what this chapter is about. It is to accentuate the variable of you. It is also to introduce concepts that will accentuate the reality of the need to do right as opposed to doing wrong. This does not mean that we have to be perfect or that ramifications due to wrong decisions cannot be changed.

However, it does mean that we have to make a true commitment to be the best parent that we can be. In the context of being a role model as a parent, you have the ability to imprint as no one else can. It is an awesome truth that is meant to bring great benefit.

Separation and Blended Families

In today's society, due to so many reasons, parents may be separated or divorced. As a result, we have shared custody in many cases, as well as blended families. Herein, I feel it is important to share a few things that will help in regarding these scenarios.

First, it is important to see things from your children's eyes. You know them better than anyone else. Communicate with them according to their individual strengths and weaknesses, according to their needs. Second, provide an environment that is predictable to ensure a mindset of safety within them.

Third, know that as you as a parent simply love your child as you always have, it will be enough. Your love will be enough. When a non-bio parent is integrated into the household, there should be appropriate transition and communication. Relationship is a process and time is on your side. The three keys are as follows. They include unity in expectations, discipline, and interaction.

Impartial love and commitment has to be shown forth daily. There will be many opportunities to show forth this commitment and love. Lastly, the non-bio parent has to be confident in who he or she is. When you are confident in who you are and in your love for the children you are now helping to parent, who you are will be imprinted upon their hearts. However, it is important to keep in mind that love is first patient!

Mom and Dad

I have just emphasized the need for unity regarding blended families. However, it is a key to any family. Unity in decision making is both a key to your children's success and safety and to your marriage relationship as well. Agreement is a powerful force. This is because it promotes both commitment and esteem.

It promotes commitment due to the perceived need agreed upon being important to the place of action. It promotes esteem due to both parents being involved and valuing one another's input. Agreement can involve process and dual compromise. However, it always should involve valuing one another's input.

If one spouse says that they really do not care what decision is made, this is not true agreement. True agreement involves involvement in both strategy and the realization of it. True agreement benefits children in many ways. First, it conveys equality in the marriage relationship. Second, it conveys to your children that they cannot manipulate you in getting one parent to side with them against the other.

Unfortunately, this is very prevalent due to the often lack of agreement in different areas. Very simply, when there is only one signal sent and not two or three, it makes it easier to understand what is permissible and what is not. Red lights mean stop and green lights mean go every day. They don't mean one thing one day and another thing another day. This helps most people to drive correctly.

Agreement will help your children do right as well. However, there will still be some manipulation, just like when you went through a light and told the officer you were sure that it was yellow, your children will say the same!

You Cannot Assume

In our last focus point of not assuming, I want to reiterate the reality of you having the ability to set the agenda regarding vision for your children. Too often, parents let other people or entities, including society itself to mold their children. Parents love their children greatly and many times work two jobs to provide for them.

They assume that the school district, the community environment, the scout leader, the coach and your neighbor's children will all be a catalyst to what you want them to be.

It is important that we do not assume. This is especially true in today's society. Very simply, you cannot assume that other people or entities are on the same page that you are on regarding what you want your children to be.

They may have an entirely different set of standards than you do. In my initial year on a local school board, I learned a very valuable lesson regarding assumption. I was put on the building committee, which included helping to monitor proposed construction projects and on-going projects. I was first involved in an engineering study to approve the architect's recommendations for an addition to one building and an upgrade for another.

It was seemingly a formality with little discussion. We were given the proposed expenditures correlative to the specific work to be done. We would approve it the following week. I took the information home and simply looked it over. Accordingly, I contacted the owner of a large company regarding the necessity of an item that was over 100,000 dollars. He felt that it was completely unnecessary and told me right away.

Consequently, I brought this issue up and the engineer without batting an eye said ok, we can scratch that off the list. I couldn't believe it. I assumed that he would make his case in a strong manner, but he did not. With a few cases, well over 150,00 dollars was saved. I learned that it payed to investigate things that most do not. In another incident, we were to make a payment to a contractor for completing a portion of a project.

It was apparent to me that the work had definitely not been completed! How could that be? Due to this situation and others, an individual was hired to make sure that the contract was being followed appropriately. I shared this with a university president a while ago and he shared this. He said that we had to hire a man to oversee things as well for quite a bit of money.

Then, we had to hire a man for more money to oversee the guy that was doing the overseeing! It proves a point, you cannot assume that your vision for your children will come about without your oversight. As shared prior, it is unfortunate but many individuals and some school districts, colleges along with some government initiatives are to instill their vision. Please never forget this. If you do not instill a vision into your children, somebody else will.

When I think of instilling a vision into their children, I think of the mother of Dr. Ben Carson and his brother. She was raising two boys by herself in an extremely difficult environment. It was difficult in the context of safety, education, and economically. She could have easily succumbed to fear and simply trying to survive.

Instead, through the power of vision, she caused the environmental giants to bow to her! The primary vision of Mrs. Carson was academic excellence. This included a regimen of study after school, instilling a love for learning and vision casting regarding the fruits of academic excellence.

The vision of Mrs. Carson for her children was not without challenges, especially as a single woman with a limited income. However, she was committed to the vision for her children. The vision certainly brought success to her children.

I vividly remember listening to Dr. Carson share a commencement address at a nearby college. It was shortly after he successfully separated twins that were co-joined.

It was the first such surgery that was successful and it saved their lives. When he spoke, he conveyed an enthusiasm for learning that was contagious. Perhaps even more importantly, he spoke of the power of vision in the life of an individual, a family and even a nation.

Again, I cannot overestimate the importance and privilege of you establishing your heart vision for your children.

Chapter 9

Love

In this text, one of the things that is most revealing is all that is involved regarding safety and the commitment that is necessary to obtain it. Truly, the key is commitment. However, the root of commitment is love. Love causes one to see things in a very powerful way. It does not see the responsibilities regarding safety as an inconvenience, but a privilege.

Love is what makes everything work. I have shared on its power prior, but I want to accentuate various traits of love as we near the end of this text.

It is all about relationship. Innately, your children are in need of your love and interaction. You do not have to fight for significance in their lives. You have it! In their hearts and their vulnerability, they are in need of who you are to them. It is love that causes who you are to your children to be realized.

Unconditional Love

A parent loves their child because of who they are, not on what they accomplish. One of the keys to parenting is being able to guide our children through the various areas of development that all will go through. Inevitably, there will be times when your children will make mistakes. There are times when they will struggle with their identity, with their self-concept. What is the key?

It is for you to be strong for your child during his or her development. All too often, it is about what children can do for their parents. It is not just wanting them to succeed for them, but to fill a void of need regarding one's own self-concept. I know that this is strong, but it needs to be addressed.

As a parent, you give strength to your children by giving them yourself. This giving is not to be periodical but daily. Very simply, being with our children should be a joy that causes us to run to our children. This joy from being with them is not a result of their measuring up to specific expectations, but a result of perceiving their personage relationally.

Children know when they are loved for who they are as opposed to being loved for what they do. A while ago, I counseled a young man who was struggling with depression. He was 15 years old and in 9th grade. He had a difficult relationship with his parents since middle school. This was due to his struggling with depression back then and his parents simply thinking that he was being lazy.

They changed their attitude in degree but "Don" still felt the sting of his parents not standing with him. In the fall of his 9th grade year, something happened that changed Don's life. He had not obtained great grades in middle school, in part due to his struggle with depression. However, due to his scoring high on a standardized test at the end of his 8th grade year, he was tested for the gifted class.

He did extremely will, easily qualifying for the gifted program. However, after being notified that he had been identified as gifted, he entered into depression. Herein, his parents contacted me. They were perplexed as they assumed that his being labeled as gifted would have the opposite effect.

I talked with Don privately (his parents were in the other room) and this was his story. He shared that when his parents were informed of his new found gifted label, they treated him totally different. It was as if he now was much more valuable in their eyes. He cried as he shared this.

I did my best to help him regarding this situation and then met with the parents by themselves. I did not immediately convey to them what was going on and simply asked them this question. Now that you know that your son is very gifted, is he now more valuable to you? Mom began to cry and rightfully so. She got the message. To my great surprise the dad hesitated and then said, I guess not.

To be very honest, I have very little tolerance for conditional love. Herein, I said this to the dad, "when you stop guessing and make a decision on why you truly value your son, it is then that he will truly feel valued."

To the father's credit, he did make a decision that opened up true relationship with his son. The father's hesitation and response broke my heart. I can only imagine what it did to that 15-year-old boy.

On the other hand, one can see the power of unconditional love. It does that which nothing else can. Someone might ask, what does this have to do with protecting our children? What does this have to do with safety? It has everything to do with protecting our children. Protecting our children does not simply involve physical safety, it involves the safeguarding of our children's emotions.

Love, unconditional love cultivates and empowers. It causes our children to know that they do not have to fight for acceptance and value.

Patience, Belief, and Hope

Love involves being patient with our children. Patience involves working with your children unto a desired end even when there is difficulty in doing so. This includes the areas of physical, emotional, intellectual, and moral development.

Physical Development

Our children develop physically at different rates. During this time of development, it is imperative that we cover our children. This is because others can be so cruel. Too short, too tall, too thin, too fat. This can be a very difficult time for our children.

During these times, our children can go through periods of inferiority and self-degradation. Consequently, during these times, they need us to be patient with their struggles. They also need a great deal of affirmation as it is so powerful, especially when anorexia and bulimia are at record highs

Emotional Development

As adults most of us are still learning to deal with emotions! This is because they are a challenge. How much more should we be patient with our children as that learn to deal with their emotions as they develop?

Many times, our children are not aware of the power of the emotions that they are dealing with. Whether it is a 2nd grader whose friend doesn't want to sit with them in the cafeteria, to puberty to failing at something, strong emotions can be elicited.

When these emotions are elicited, things can be said by our children that they do not mean. They can be moody and struggle. As well, emotions can lead the feet of our children into places that they should not be in. Herein, guidelines need to be set, but as parents we need to not simply endure that time, we need to walk with them during this time.

Academic Development

As with other areas, our children need support regarding academic development. A few keys to help in developing this area are as follows.

Start Early

It is very important to interact with your child intellectually from birth. It is remarkable, for example how the first five years of a child's life intellectual development can affect the rest of their development. I know that I have said this different times, but it is so very important.

Love of Learning

It is of course very significant to have your child be academically proficient. However, it is also so very important to instill in our children a love of learning. It is one thing to obtain knowledge. It is another thing to understand how exciting it is to be able to grow intellectually and to utilize knowledge to solve problems.

This includes personal problem solving as well as that which helps meet the needs of others. Truly, when one sees the power of learning and the doors that it can open, there is an excitement that comes. This excitement causes your child to appreciate the privilege to learn. It also will cause your child to excel in all of that which he or she pursues.

No Comparisons

All of our children are gifted in different ways. One may gravitate towards proficiency regarding auto mechanics. Others may lean toward nursing or teaching. It is wrong to elevate one above another. We need to esteem all giftings and encourage the cultivation of these giftings.

We have shared on the variable of comparison prior, but it bears repetition. We need to have zero tolerance in this area of comparison as it can be so harmful.

Consistent Reinforcement

Our children need our reinforcement in the various stages of their academic development. As with anything, there will be ups and downs. They may do great with Algebra and struggle with Geometry. They may do great in English but not in Science.

Accordingly, our children need to be reinforced. They need to be reinforced for both their efforts and achievements. This reinforcement causes them to see that their efforts are being appreciated and mean much to you. Success is key to all of us. Success breeds success. This is why as parents, we are to celebrate the successes of our children.

Again, success is to include our children's efforts and accomplishments. We are to work with them to help their academic weaknesses and to accentuate their academic strengths. Everyone needs encouragement and reinforcement, this is especially true regarding our children.

Moral Development

Morals, what you consider right living is that which has to be developed. It is wise to start this development early. Your children are in need of your helping them in this area. Morality simply does not happen naturally. Teaching, guidance, and patience are necessary ingredients in developing this area.

Regarding this area a book called "Driving Through Shreveport" is a great read. The book chronicles how two brothers made it to the major league in baseball. However, more importantly, it shares how their parents imparted moral fiber to their sons that enabled them to endure various challenges unto success.

Both boys were very good players from 2nd grade on. However, they were taught to never be prideful and to respect all players, no matter what their talent level was. From 2nd grade to high school, their dad asked them to clean out the dugout after each game as a part of servanthood. They were taught to run through outs and to be team players.

They were also taught to never give up, no matter what challenges that they would face. These traits that were instilled enabled them to not only succeed in baseball but in life. Again, moral attributes simply do not happen. They need to be both instilled and cultivated. The following are the seven areas of morality that build a foundation for our children in this area.

Equality

There truly is no one that is created better than anyone else. Herein, there is never any room for racism, prejudice, and degradation of any kind.

Compassion

Raising children to be compassionate and wanting to help others is a key to society. This compassion accomplishes two things. First, it helps meet the needs of those less fortunate. This can include the abused, the handicapped, the grief-stricken, and the impoverished.

Second, it does something for the one who has made meeting the needs of others a priority. It produces empathy and strength of character. It produces an unselfishness and satisfaction from putting others before themselves.

Sexual Interaction

Most nations have laws dealing with the age of consent and the need of mutual consent regarding sexual interaction. These laws of course need to be adhered to but there is much more involved in the area of sexuality. It includes respect and the esteeming or relationship.

Unfortunately, date rape is rampant today in our society. What is so sad is that the majority of those harmed by date rape were harmed by significant others. This simply should not be. Parents cannot afford in any way to make this area of morality peripheral, it has to be made a primary priority. Love entails esteeming one another in a way that regarding sexuality, all are safe.

Opioids – Alcohol – Nicotine

The opioid epidemic has harmed so many. Just last night, a precious individual who is beating the odds with the help of our counseling center shared this. She said she had lost five friends to Heroin in the last week. It is hard for me to comprehend that reality.

Alcohol is still a killer among our children. It is overly accepted and easily accessible. Concerning nicotine, there are so many new techniques that can enable massive amounts of nicotine to be consumed by our children. Many times, they do not even realize how much.

The key as parents is to be proactive in the context of our children's development regarding this area. We cannot do everything, but we have to do all that we can.

Bullying

We have discussed this area from various vantage points. Regarding morality, there simply has to be a zero-tolerance mindset. This includes physical bullying as well as mental and emotional bullying. It involves domestic violence, where men bully their wives (can be vice versa at times as well) and their children as well.

It can include work place bullying through the misuse of position. It can include bullying through misuse of authority through those in the armed forces, court system or police. With the internet, bullying can take many forms. It is imperative that parents address this area with all diligence. This includes not reinforcing it in anyway and fully standing up against it.

Fighting Through Adversity

Adversity will come to all of us, including our children. Consequently, it is vital to prepare them for challenges that will they face. It is so important for them to know that as they persevere, they will come out the other side. It is equally important for them to know that they will not be alone during this time, because you will be there.

Work Ethic

There is no substitute for a strong work ethic. This is due to the fruits of this mindset and it is a mindset. If our children do not believe that working hard will benefit them, then they will not esteem working hard. If all parents do is speak about an unlevel playing field and inopportunity, children will have a negative mindset regarding work and opportunity.

There will always be obstacles and challenges. However, it is critical to emphasize the ability to overcome them.

Again, love involves imparting to our children inward character that our society is based on. When you love someone, you want them to be strong as possible regarding their character.

Parental Responses

We have addressed some of these issues in prior chapters. However, in this chapter simply entitled love, we are adding additional wisdom keys and accentuating the need as parents to be profoundly intense regarding their role as protector.

Equality

It is easy to say that there is neither prejudice nor bigotry in us. However, we need to look deep within ourselves. Our children should never hear us degrade any people group. However, they should also hear us celebrating people regarding their efforts and contributions. I shared that this chapter on love is about going into more detail and to a greater depth regarding various variables.

With each of these 7 areas, as parents, we have to be all in. This means living to cultivate these areas. Herein, let me share 2 examples of this from my own life. The first is when my wife and I and our four children were staying in a hotel while on vacation. During this time, the kids and I were simply being way too messy with garbage in the room.

One of us after spilling something that was sticky said, "oh don't worry about it, the maid will take care of it." When this comment was made, I saw immediately how we were treating the maid with disrespect and degrading her. It is one thing for her to help clean the room. It is entirely another thing to cause her to assume responsibilities that she should not have to.

My wife and I used it as a teachable moment regarding true equality. Why would we treat her like that? Would we want to be treated like that? The children responded well, we actually got to converse with her and leave a small tip to encourage her. Our children are now older, but still remember that experience.

The second example revolves around a young man from Africa (Liberia) whose name was Moo Moo. We were renting a large house at the time in a college community. We housed 7 students from Africa in the upstairs for a very minimal fee to help them. I would never thought I would have any prejudice (pre-judgments) towards any of these guys. However, I had an experience that proved otherwise.

The guys showered downstairs in our basement. It was not the greatest but was ok. I thought to myself, these guys will not mind because it is probably better than what they are used to. Shortly after that Moo Moo came to talk to me. He asked if he could clean up the shower area to make it both safer and cleaner. It was not what he was used to.

Just prior to this, one of the students from Malawi (Southern Africa) shared with me that his sister spoke seven languages fluently. I was really surprised. I put these two responses together in my mind and realized how prejudice I was. I had made my opinion of these students due to my limited frame of reference. I had labeled them as not as concerned about facilities to wash in and speaking several languages as not in their educational paradigm.

I just wept for about 20 minutes. My oldest daughter saw me and asked me what was wrong. Consequently, I shared with her. I then apologized to these young men for my ignorance in judging them wrongly.

A third example where prejudice was in me that I did not realize involved a young man struggling with Heroin addiction. He had been struggling for about 6 months and I was trying to help him. Unfortunately, instead of dealing with him as an individual, I prejudged him very wrongly. My mindset was that he simply wanted to be rebellious, did not want to take responsibility, and just needed to try harder.

This was until one day, he shared his heart saying, "do you really think that I chose to struggle with this?" He shared with me of an older cousin who sexually abused him for years and then after threatening him brought some Heroin over. He was so messed up emotionally that he did Heroin with him (being so used to doing what he wanted) several times.

Now, he was having a tough time getting off it, wow, so much for my mindset regarding him. Well, I wept again and vowed to not prejudge someone like him. I have had so many parents tell me, "I thought those that struggled with addiction were just rebellious and dirty." This was until my child struggled with addiction.

There is a balance, decisions have to be made. However, more often than not, there is more than meets the eye. I have shared these personal examples because it is so easy to not be all that we should be in regarding these various areas that effect our children's development. It is when they see things such as equality meaning so much to us, it will then mean much to them.

Academics

We have shared how this area of development greatly effects our children regarding their self-concept. This is because it is one of societies greatest gauges regarding success and identity. Herein, it is important to help our children do their best academically. However, it is equally important that we do not let their academic performance define them.

My wife and I have good friends who have 4 children. The oldest is a medical doctor and unmarried at this time. He is a great young man. Their second child is a teacher and just recently married. Her third child is a full-time mom. She and her husband have 3 awesome children. Their youngest child works in the produce section of a major grocery store chain. He is also a part-time Pastor at his church.

All of their children have different gifts and degrees of academic proficiency. They are all awesome!

Again, as parents we need to have a goal of academic excellence for each of our children. Accordingly, we need to expect them to make a strong effort. However, we need to see that everyone is different. Society may say that being a doctor is better than being in another vocation such as being a truck driver. This is so unfair and wrong. Vocation and value are in no way fully correlated.

Compassion through Experience

Experience is a powerful teacher. It is so easy to say that we understand something or someone, but really not understand. I know that they have it bad but in the back of your mind, we minimize how bad someone has it. I know that I should not send that text that puts that person down, but it isn't that big of a deal. I know that I should be more thankful, but I am more thankful than most.

Regarding the latter, Tonya ha a life changing experience through her mom's use of a challenging experience. Tonya was 13 at the time and was in a complaining stage. This was due to comparing herself with other friends who materially, had more than her.

Her mom, a single mom simply could not provide certain things that her friends had. However, she was an awesome mom and signed her and Tonya up to visit a children's hospital to volunteer with young children in need of a visit.

It was a life changing experience for Tonya. She did not want to go but was so glad that her mom scheduled the visits. It was life changing due to seeing the challenges of the children and their amazing attitude changed her. Tonya, now 17 and applying for nursing schools in hopes of working with young children fighting the most difficult situations one could imagine.

I want to emphasize two things regarding this scenario. First, her mom was very intentional regarding having her daughter volunteer with her at the hospital. She saw a need in her daughter's life and did something about it. She simply did not hope that something would change. She became an agent of change through being intentional.

Second, there was no guarantee that her idea would help her daughter. However, she felt that it had a good chance of impacting her in a very positive way. If this has not worked, she would have found something else that had a good chance of working.

When we find possible solutions for our children, there is a good chance that possibility becomes a true solution.

Tonya's mom did not have her volunteer with her just to get her to stop complaining. She did it to help her daughter grow into the person that she was meant to be. This is what love is all about.

Chapter 10

Coronavirus 19

It is imperative that we address the Corona Virus with our children. As with virtually all areas of safety, communication is an absolute must. We want to be proactive in regards to discerning how the pandemic can affect our children and how to help them through it.

I believe that the wisdom intrinsic to the following variables will be of significant help to you in this regard.

Communications

As a parent, it is up to you to initiate the communication necessary to meet the needs of your children.

Many times, we as parents will communicate when we see our children being hurt or when they bring an issue that concerns them to our attention.

168

However, we need to communicate pre-emptively before our children are harmed. Harm can include fear, depression, personality changes and a lack of confidence due to unsurity.

Regarding you child, whether 3 years old or 22 years old, one can not assume that because they do not initiate. Communication that there is not a need for it. Our children need their parents to give them the opportunity to convey that which they are dealing with.

Know Your Child

I have shared the significance of this variable prior, but want to emphasize it again in regards to the Corona Virus.

Every child will act different in regard to the Corona Virus. This is due to the difference in personalities, age, and life experiences.

Let us look at a family, that has 3 children, Thomas is 16, Julie is 14, and Johnny is 12.

Thomas seems to be struggling with the pandemic but says that he simply does not want to talk about it. He has been in a gifted class since 5th grade (now in tenth grade) and looks at most things from a very intellectual viewpoint. He has great respect for his teachers, especially Dr. Smith, who is in charge of his high school gifted program.

Unbeknown to his parents, Dr. Smith emphatically told Tom that the Corona Virus is akin to the Spanish Flu of 1918. It will kill millions, especially when it comes back in the winter. This of course is his opinion and should never been shared so emphatically with Tom. However, it really has affected him adversely.

Julie is fourteen and finishing eighth grade. She seems unaffected by the pandemic. She is as happy-go-lucky as before and seems to be little affected by what is going on around her. Her parents, dad especially sees this as a sign of strength.

Johnny is twelve and is just finishing 6th grade. He was diagnosed with mild depression in 5th Grade and takes much to heart. This is a strength, but also can be a weakness.

He sees the Corona Virus in the context of his elementary school principal having the virus and is fearful. He is fearful to the point where he is constantly washing his hands in an obsessive manner. His dad, unfortunately, sees this as a weakness that he just needs to get over.

False Comparison

Regarding these scenarios, two things have to take place. First, the parents have to stop making false comparison. This includes general comparisons to these of children their age in general and in comparison within the family.

Julie is not stronger or better than her siblings due to her seeming calm and happy-go-lucky behavior. This is simply her personality and you cannot even be sure that she is not struggling.

Communication

Second, there needs to be time spent with each child individually and then together. Questions need to be asked in genuine concern.

Thomas desperately needs to share of being triggered by Dr. Smith and given help in dealing with it.

Julie needs to know that it is ok not to always feel she has to be strong. It is ok to share of that which is bothering her. However, it is not ok to call her younger brother weak or even a big baby because she hears him crying in his bedroom. Johnny needs to be assured that it is alright to cry and they believe he is strong. He needs to be given coping skills and have time with his parents daily to talk.

Again, we need to stay away from comparison: we also need to understand that communication is a necessity even when it seems like it is unnecessary.

Age

When communicating with your child, the ages of your child needs to be considered. Accordingly, let us look at the age of 3. 8. 13, & 18 in regard to appropriate communication.

Three Years Old

A three old child needs to be communicated with in a very concrete matter. This is due to his or her abstract thinking, being in an initial stage of development.

For example, you do not want to try to explain the intricacies associated with the Corona Virus. You want to communicate on their level in regard to that which is both observable and understandable.

That which is observance is the face mask that they have to wear when in different environments. e.g. stores, daycare, church, or at grandma's house.

They need you to have a good attitude towards the masks. They need you to relate to them as they are able to hear, All children, especially 3 to 6 years old need reinforcement.

One simple act of reinforcement is modeling. Parents need to wear masks as required just as they are asking their child to meet requirements.

As well, simple ways to connect with the child should be utilized. This can include making masks with your little one and or having them pick out the color that they like best for their mask.

As well, even at this early age of three, the variable of knowing your child comes into play. For example, if your day care requires a child at the age of 3 wear a mask the entire day and you know that this is unrealistic for your child, do what you need to do. It may be less hours at the day care each day, going just a few days, or not at all.

You know your child better than anytime else and have the freedom to do whatever is in his or her best interests.

8-Years-Old

When a child is at this age, they have the ability to understand more. However, they are still not at the age where you can interact with them inductively.

Consequently, you have to set boundaries for their safety and interact with them in a very structured way.

For example, you can share with them through simple analogies. You can share how they felt when they had a fever and felt sick. You can then share That we are staying inside more or wearing a mask in school to protect us from being sick.

At this age, it is important for you to ask questions and to let them know that they can talk to you if they are afraid of something.

Some questions that can be asked can be similar to these:

1. When you are at school, does anyone of your friends not wear a mask?

2. At school, do any of the adults not wear a mask?

3. Did anyone say that they liked your mask?

4. Did anyone of your friends offer you something to eat from their

plate? What did you do ?

5. Is everything ok? Are you looking forward to school today?

Questions promote interaction. Questions from you also cause your child to feel comfortable in asking you questions.

Modeling is again a key and a positive attitude goes a long way as well. An eight-year-old to those who are ten and eleven are very dependent upon your leadership.

13 year-olds to 16

A young teenager needs your interaction so very much, especially those up to 16 years of age. This is because their sphere of contacts is now increasing. Accordingly, they are now being presented with different scenarios that need to be addressed.

They are transitioning from elementary school to junior high and from junior high to high school. They have an ability to perceive what others are thinking about them and internalize these perceptions in a very strong way.

Consequently, it is critical not to dismiss the need for interaction with you even though they are becoming more independent.

In this age group, it is important to remember that identity is still being formed during this time. Your child is in the process of discovering who they are, their purpose and talents. It can be a volatile time as confidence levels can fluctuate with either positive or negative reinforcement.

Peer Pressure

Herein, peer pressure is a very significant variable in the lives of this age group. Consequently, it is very important that you encourage your child to have beneficial peer relationships and help him or her to evaluate these relationships. Does their closest peer groups honor mandated guidelines of facemasks and social distancing? Does their peer relationships respect their mindsets or pressure them to do that which is not right?

You will only know what is going on in this area if you interact with your teenager and make it a priority to do so.

Abstract Thinking – Why?

In this age group, abstract thinking is at a higher level than ever before. With this reality now present and coupled with a search for identity, many questions arise. Why did Jimmy's dad die? Why does Grandma now have to go through the quarantine process? Why is there so much suffering around us?

It is important as a parent to not quench this season of questioning, not to minimize your teenager's need for answers. You are busy. You are tired. You have financial pressures. Herein, it is so easy to see their question as an inconvenience rather than the opportunity of a lifetime. Very simply, if you are not there to answer their questions, someone else who does not have the best intentions in mind might. Again, being involved in your child's discovery process as a teen is both a responsibility and a privilege.

Knowing Your Child

We have emphasized this variable in our prior age groups and will do so again. Very simply, it is so significant that you do not assume that your child is like everyone else. For example, your son may be a very good wrestler. Everyone on his team seems to be thrilled that the season will go on. However, you notice that your son is not excited about the upcoming season. You can talk to him or just assume that it is no big deal.

However, when you talk to him, you find out that he is fearful of wrestling again due to the pandemic. You find out that it is because a friend of his that he met at a wrestling camp from New York City has contracted the virus and is not doing well.

Now that you know this, you can help him understanding that it is different for him, living in Florida, than where this young man from camp is from. You can share that you will honor his decision to do what he feels comfortable with. You can be a strength to him that he needs during this time.

Again, every child is different and has different areas of need. You are a primary vehicle of these needs being met.

At times, it can also involve someone else to help in different situations. This can be a counselor, a friend of his, a youth pastor, or someone else who is significant to him or her.

Offensive Mindset

One of the negatives of self-isolation is that one can enter into a defensive posture in life. Defense is good, but it is also essential to be proactive. During this time of adjustment and transition, it is important to make life what you want it to be.

For example, you and your children can help out at the local food bank. You might make cards for the elderly in nursing homes. You might organize a virtual race to raise money for the families of those hurt by the virus. You might make masks with your family for veterans and as restrictions are lifted, you can visit those in need.

It can make a tremendous difference in the life of your child and in the lives of those you help.

17-22 years old

When our children are in this age group, it is easy to not communicate with them as we should. This is due to their being more independent and our thinking that they do not need us as much as prior. From working with this age group in a college setting for decades, I can tell you that they need you more than ever before.

This is due to their facing situations that they have never faced before. This is especially true in the time of a pandemic that is worldwide.

It is important to note that in this age group, identity is still being formed. As well, expectations regarding college and vocational success is at a premium. This is of also course a time where dating relationships unto commitment are being realized for many. Consequently, there is pressure to meet expectations as never before. These expectations can be either good or bad.

Group Activities

Just yesterday, I was walking on a track owned by a university in ,y home town. As I was walking, I looked up and saw about 20 young people in this age group (17-22) partying. They were in no wise thinking about social distancing. Some seemed to be drinking from the same bottle (beer) and passing it around.

It was obvious that there was pressure to join the party despite endangering themselves due to the COVID -19 pandemic. This is where open communication with your child is significant. They need to share with you what is going on. They need you to ask them what is going on.

What if they know they should not be involved in this behavior, but may not know how to get out of it. What happens if one of their friends gets the virus due to this interaction and they feel responsible? This is real life and counseling situations I deal with over and over again. They need to know that communication is open with you, that you care and that you will not belittle them, but extend your heart unto them.

Vocation

Your son or daughter may be 22 years-old, but struggling with fear in some way regarding the virus. They may know of a high school teacher that caught COVID-19 and their student teaching assignment is in this high school.

They may have to do an internship to complete their nursing degree in a large hospital or in a nursing home and are having second thoughts. They need your love, your counsel and your understanding. It is times like these that your children will always remember when you help them. This is what legacy is all about.

Specific Challenges-Quarantine

As you know from regarding this book, I am very big on sharing both practical experiences and possible scenarios applicable to conveying various principles.

Here is a scenario. Your daughter is a very good volleyball player. One of her best friends and teammates is told by her family physician that she needs to be quarantined for two weeks. This is due to her having been at a home where the mother of her friend tested positive for COVID – 19.

She shares this with your daughter and nobody else. The championship game is in just 3 days. They are both seniors and this is their dream contest. She says that she will start the quarantine the day after the championship.

What does your daughter do? Nobody will ever know. Your daughter has promised not to share this with anyone. However, she is now in a time of great struggle emotionally. What is the key? It is communication and wisdom intrinsic to her communication with you. Someone says, "That could never happen!" Really? You cannot control scenarios that your child, young or old, will encounter. However, you can establish a paradigm of communication that enables your little one or college senior to utilize in their time of need.

Nobody asked for this pandemic. However, we must be ready for it in the context of relationship and communication. It may not be convenient and may stretch you as a parent. However, this is what true parenting is all about.

Self-Examination as Parents

The Corona Virus pandemic has called all of us to be stretched in some way or another. Domestic abuse and addiction of every kind has doubled and tripled in the United States. As well, many adults are struggling, with great depression, anger, and discord. It does not have to affect you in this manner. What is the provision?

The provision entails 3 variables. First, we have to make a decision to deal with the challenges that the COVID-19 presents. In every situation, you can either choose to get better or be bitter.

I am not saying that it is a piece of cake. However, our attitude can make al the difference. Second, as parents we need to understand that the different pressures associated with this pandemic can cause weaknesses to come to the surface.

You thought you were patient with your children until you had to homeschool them and spend 16 hours a day with them! You never would think of raising your voice to your spouse and belittle them until they tell you that during the stay-at-home order you are expected to paint the house, put a new fence around that yard, and build a deck! You never thought you would struggle with consuming alcohol in a bad way until your pay check can no longer cover your mortgage. When wrongful behaviors surface, it is not a time to hide from them or run from them. It is a time to accept the reality that there are issues within you that need to be dealt with.

Third, it is important to understand that with every issue that has surfaced, there is a solution. You may find the solution in a deeper relationship with your spouse or with talking to a counselor you can trust. The solution may be in your relationship with God and your relationship with those of like beliefs. The solution may be in simply making a decision to make a greater effort regarding the situation or in an attitude adjustment. The provision may be motivational, in seeing how much your family needs you and or how much you have to be thankful for.

Again, you can choose to get better or bitter regarding the pandemic. When you choose to be better, it is of benefit to all.

General Interaction – Judging Rightly in Love

The following subject is very significant regarding the raising of our children and in establishing good relationships.

The COVID-19 pandemic has caused a sharp divide among people, even among families. This divide involves the validity of the virus, how the virus came about, will the virus come back like the Spanish Flu of 1918, and how politicians may have contrived this virus to control people. The list goes on and on.

Now, the balance is that you have a right to have your opinion. You have a right to share truth that is absolutely apparent. For example, I find it difficult to understand how authorities can give tickets to those at a drive-in church service where there is absolutely no interaction between people. You can not catch the virus due to someone else's car touching your bumper.

The following are very realistic scenarios that exemplify real mindsets. These mindsets are not necessarily valid at all.

Virus Really Not Valid, Few People Affected

I want you to understand that the mindsets shared are by good people who are as a whole very smart people. As well, it should be noted that as with any mindset, there are stats used to validate their position. To complicate things, the experts who usually try their best have changed their positions on potential cases, deaths, and rationales for shout downs over and over again.

Jimmy is 12 years old. His parents are professional people, one being a professor at a very reputable college. They have shared with Jimmy their views and he adopts these views readily.

One of his 6th grade classmates shares with him online that his mom has the virus and is in the hospital. Jimmy's quick reply is that she probably really doesn't have it and it is not something to be concerned about. His friend is very upset and shares that he is not allowed to talk to Jimmy again. Jimmy is confused.

The issue here is two-fold. The first is that we need to teach our children the difference between our opinions (which at times may be right) and the reality of other mindsets being very viable.

Second, we have to teach our children to be sensitive to the needs of others. This 6th grade friend of Jimmy's was in a very vulnerable state emotionally. It was not the time to make the focus the opinion regarding the validity of his mom's condition. It is so important to consider not just what our opinion is, but even more important what it will do to the person that may be in a very vulnerable state.

Hazard Pay

I know 2 individuals that both own essential businesses (these men know each other). The first has given each of his 25 employees two dollars an hour hazard pay raises. The other man chose not to do this as he feels it would cause him to have to lay off employees to do so.

Some may see the man giving the raise as a better man. I am not going to be their judge. They are both worthy of respect. However, the man that did not give the raises said that he has been put down by different friends. In my opinion, they are both doing their best.

Wimps and Cowards?

Recently, a man that I believe genuinely cares about people as a minister said something that shocked me. He conveyed that people who wear masks are wimps and cowards as Christians.

I try to see the perspective of a person regarding different mindsets regarding the virus. The man seems to have strong faith and is to be commended for that. However, just because someone chooses to wear a mask as the government ask does not mean that they don't have faith and deserve to be degraded. People are already going through enough. They need to be understood where they are at and not condemned.

Emotions

In a pandemic, emotions can run high. You may be right in what you think. However, being right does not give you the right to put your righteousness above the value of a person. With some who are strong, it is certainly ok to share what you think. However, in the midst of a pandemic we need to meet the needs of others above our conveying that we are right.

In this context, we need to go over possible scenarios with our children that they may very well face. Doing this will prepare your child for that which will enable them to live in wisdom.

Conclusion

We have covered a lot in this chapter. To conclude, I want to encourage you to see that this is a time that your children will always remember. It is a time to establish legacy.

Although, the pandemic brings with it different challenges, it is a time of opportunity. It is a time to spend more time with your spouse and children. It is a time to grow in your own character. It is a time to help those who are in great need.

This can be through lending a listening ear, praying for someone, volunteering at the food bank, and comforting someone who has been affected adversely by the virus.

Life can be challenging at times. However, as we and our children proactively engage the challenges, we will come out the other side stronger than ever before.

Chapter 11

Composite

In this chapter, I want to share a simple platelet with you that will enable you to organize some of the information shared regarding both you and your child or children. This information can then be easily referenced when you are making decisions that affect your child or children.

In today's society, advertisers acquire information about you so they know what products you will mostly buy and how to market it.

Major league baseball teams obtain information about every hitter in the league so they know what pitches are to be thrown to them and where. It is so much more important to develop a family composite to know how we can best meet the needs of our children and to keep them safe. It is important to write this composite out and keep it at the forefront of your mind.

The composite that will be shared revolves around 3 simple areas. They first include knowing your child, yourself, and your family history. Second, it involves knowing the environment that you and your child are presented with. Third, it involves making the decisions that cause your child to grow most and be the safest within this environment

Child

Name _____

Date of Birth _____

4 Main strengths _____

_____

3 Main Weakness _____

_____

Personality Types (e.g. outgoing, shy, dominant)

*There are numerous personality tests that can be easily obtained and administered.

Love Language (from book *Love Language for Children* by Gary Chapman)

Verbal affirmation, gifts, acts of service, touch, and quality time

<u>Child</u>

Scale of 1-10, 10 being the highest:

_____ Definite risk taker

_____ Responds well to confrontation

_____ Does not fear rejection

_____ Deals well when given constructive criticism

_____ Is able to handle failure well (doesn't let it devastate or

define him or her)

_____ Not predisposed to addiction

_____ Does not struggle with depression

_____ Is a team player, works well with others

_____ Loves to learn

_____ Problem solver

_____ Cares about others much

_____ Is hurt greatly when unjustly treated

_____ Would rather follow than lead

_____ Has very high expectations

_____ Cares about what others think too much

_____ Totally self-motivated

_____ Confident in herself or himself

_____ Does not get angry easily

_____ Is very positive in general

_____ Chooses friends that are good for him or her

Parents

Scale of 1-10, 10 being the highest:

_____ Definite risk taker

_____ Responds well to confrontation

_____ Does not fear rejection

_____ Deals well when given constructive criticism

_____ Is able to handle failure well (doesn't let it devastate or define him or her)

_____ Not predisposed to addiction

_____ Does not struggle with depression

_____ Is a team player, works well with others

_____ Loves to learn

_____ Problem solver

_____ Cares about others much

_____ Is hurt greatly when unjustly treated

_____ Would rather follow than lead

_____ Has very high expectations

_____ Cares about what others think too much

_____ Totally self-motivated

_____ Confident in herself or himself

_____ Does not get angry easily

_____ Is very positive in general

_____ Chooses friends that are good for him or her

_____ Supports spouse (if applicable) in regard to disciple

_____ Shows no partiality towards one particular child

_____ Models well that which you tell your child to do

_____ Is positive towards _____ (spouses name) in front of child

_____ Speaks positive about child to others

Family Dynamics

Number of children: _____

Birth order: _____

_____

Family History

Family history is significant in that it causes us to be aware of possible predispositions in both ourselves and our children.

Sickness

We see family history increasingly used in the medical field. Utilizing family medical history, specific trends are seen and then translated into probability regarding specific diseases.

Policies of the School your Children Attend

This is a major part of your composite due to its impact on your child. School policy is so very vital. It involves bullying, drug use, field trips, sexual harassment, graduation requirements, drugs, attendance and so much more. Whatever is important to you should be communicated in school policy.

Curriculum

I am surprised at the number of parents who are unsure of what the curriculum that entails that their children use. Very simply, I think that we need to know curriculum emphasis regarding specific subjects. Accordingly, it is wise to look at the books that your children use.

History

History books are no longer what many would think. It used to be that freshmen had State History, sophomores U.S. History and Juniors World History, and Seniors taking an elective.

Text books are published by various companies. For decades, they were similar in their accounts of U.S. involvement in World War I, Worlds War II, the Korean War, and other conflicts.

However, different publishers now share abbreviated information regarding the wars. As a school board member, I was surprised to learn that some portray the United States in a less than positive fashion.

Different schools have adopted this modified view of the United States. Many others have continued to keep a more unaltered curriculum.

The bottom line is that it is critical to evaluate the curriculum of the school and then monitor what is taking place in class.

Individual Needs

This is a very important part of the school environment. So often, parents line up to what is available in a school system rather than being selective.

Every child has specific needs based on giftings, weaknesses, and interests. The days when only one option existed educationally are over. One size fits all is not acceptable.

You as a parent know your child. Better than anyone else. Herein, it is important for you to proactively see that your child's needs are met.

Specific School Options

Various school districts are now offering specific schools within the system designed to focus on specific giftings of students.

Some of these schools include music, art, drama, vocational technical, language, and entrepreneurial. This is tremendous. While teaching, I saw that there were many students who were very gifted in regards to auto mechanics, auto body, cosmetology, and drafting. Unfortunately, many of these students were not given the opportunity to attend a school that fit them.

Worst of all, they were given courses not only not correlative to their strengths, they were many times put down, even degraded. Thankfully, things are changing.

Academics

The quality of programing is not the same in every school district. Regarding academics in general or regarding special needs.

Gifted

If you have a child who is gifted, you want to have a school that provides quality gifted instruction. You need to find out when the program starts and what it consists of.

As well, with college prep students, you want to know what the ratings are for your school. As well, does the school enable your child to obtain college credits through a co-operative program with a higher education institution?

Special Education

If your child has an academic weakness such as Dyslexia, lower I.Q., ADD, general learning disability or autism, you need to evaluate the ability of the district to meet that need. Sometimes, just talking to another parent who has a child in similar circumstances can be beneficial.

Activities

Activities are important to a student. Activities can include sports, drama, debate, 4-H club, forensics, key club, and jazz band.

Sports

Sports are an important part of our society. It is a very significant part of the lives of many of our children.

Herein, if it is important to them, it should be important to us as parents.

If your son plays hockey or your daughter runs cross-country or plays golf, it would be good to go to a school that has these sports!

If your child loves a sport and can play in one school district but not make the team in another, this should be considered.

As well, the quality and demeanor of the coaching staff should be considered as well.

Drama, Debate, & Forensics

I am someone who really likes sports, but all children need to be considered equally. While serving on my local school board, I was a major proponent of the arts and academic games.

I am amazed how so many districts disclude students through not offering various programs for them that would be of benefit.

Regarding forensics, very few districts make this program a priority. Consequently, many students in grades 7th-12th never get the opportunity to cultivate who they are.

I was counseling a young girl (8th grade) with her parents. She was struggling with her identity. She was a very bright young lady. I recommended her getting involved with the forensic group.

She flourished, actually winning numerous awards her freshmen year in speech. More importantly, she developed great relationship and her self-concept increased greatly.

If this was your child, would it be worth it to have her in this program? Some may ask, what does this have to do with keeping your children safe? It has much to do with safety. This is because safety is wholistic. It involves every part of us.

As with the girl mentioned just prior, her entering into finding her place intrinsic to the school system negated emotional struggles and suicidal predispositions.

Very simply, the school system of your choice should be a place that lends itself to the physical, emotional, academic, and social well-being of your child.

I firmly believe that every school should have a forensic program. In one school district it can involve up to 100 students, 7th-12th grades. If in just one state 200 schools do not have this program, we are depriving 20,000 students of a possible opportunity to establish their identity.

School Chemistry

This is a key variable regarding school safety, especially in the context of bullying and discrimination.

School chemistry is defined as how staff and students as a whole perceive one another and work together.

A school district is a lot like an individual, it develops a reputation. It can be a school that is in some ways tolerant of bullying or even racist to a degree.

It can be a school that is known for school spirit regarding all students, a school that stands up for those in need.

In one school, assemblies had to be cancelled in both the middle school and high school due to the misbehavior and rudeness of students. In another, assemblies were added due to the positive response of students.

Your children sense the type of environment that is within their school.

General Social Environment

As we leave the variable of school safety and the specific variable of school chemistry, it is a perfect segue to our next area.

The area of general social environment is multifaceted. It includes personal acceptance, social availability, laws and ordinances, potential advancement, and reputation.

Personal Acceptance

In today's society there is more diversity than ever before. From conservative and liberal to moderates and everywhere in-between, this is today's society. The key is twofold. It is to try to understand where someone else is coming from. Second, it is to know that it is ok to disagree with someone else's viewpoint. However, it is certainly not ok to be disrespectful and promote harm.

In your composite, it is imperative to be realistic. For example, if an area is known for racism and violence, and your child can be targeted accordingly, this has to be considered.

Years ago, Hall of Famer, Willie Stargell spoke at the university where I live. There was about 200 people in attendance.

He was amazing and really shared his heart. He said that while in the minor leagues, he received a death threat that if he played that night, his life would end.

With great emotion, he shared that he decided to play, even if it would cost him his life. Wow. That is really something.

However, not everyone could do what Willie Stargell did. Again, it is unfair to put your child in the midst of a racially charged environment. Unfortunately, these environments still exist.

Just recently, I met with a mom whose son and daughter-in-law were contemplating moving into a very difficult area.

They could purchase the 3-bedroom house for under 20,000 dollars. I knew that area and cautioned them regarding the purchase. They had 2 adopted children, ages 13 and 15 who were adopted just two years prior from Asia.

The parents are great and very adventurous, liking challenges. However, the young teens were not. They were not readily assimilated into the area and faced a lot of unkind experiences that they were not prepared for.

At the same time, there are many areas where they would have been treated totally different. This is why this area of acceptance should be a part of your composite.

Social Mindsets

There are many mindsets in our nation regarding various social issues. For example, in one area Marijuana may be legal and across the state illegal. How does this affect your children? If your child struggles with peer pressure or is a risk taker, this environment has to be considered.

Geographical Safety

Geographical safety entails the specific variables and entities intrinsic to the physical environment of an area. It includes climate, rate, animal and insect challenges, topography and population distribution.

Climate

This seems like a simple variable, but it can be overlooked.

Years ago, I was involved in hiring a director for an organization. Initially, she did well but began to have a hard time. She came from a very sunny part of the nation. In our area, the sun did not shine much at all. Consequently, it was very difficult for her.

We obtained for her a Therapy Lamp that produces artificial light to help her fight off seasonal depression and it did help her. However, she ended up moving to a different climate and did much better there.

As well, in an area where there is limited sun it is very necessary to add vitamin D to your diet, especially women. Vitamin D is incredibly important in this type of environment.

Air-Pollution

As shared prior, the incidence of Asthma among school age children continues to rise. If your child falls into this category, it is important to consider the pollution index that would affect this condition.

As well, different geographical areas have higher pollen counts that affect our children.

Animal and Insect Challenges

There are challenges that exist in almost every geographical area. Unfortunately, these are things that the realtor usually doesn't emphasize!

Spiders

There are a lot of spiders where I live in Pennsylvania. However, the definite majority are not poisonous.

My wife and I had friends who moved to a certain area in Florida. Both of them were bitten by spiders that were poisonous and were ill affected for many months.

They shared that they had no idea of these spiders being in the area. They were just thankful that their teenage son was not bitten. The need to be aware of your environment cannot be underestimated. It needs to be part of your decision making.

Ticks

Deer ticks that carry Lyme's Disease are very prevalent in Pennsylvania, especially in western Pennsylvania.

It is not a reason not to move to the area. However, it is certainty something that one needs to be aware of.

I personally know at least two dozen people with Lyme's Disease, including 6 teenagers. It is a very serious threat to safety.

Wild Dogs

Again, this is shared so that you are aware of your physical environment. A man I know of was excited when his son accepted a job out west.

However, less than 2 months there, while training for a triathlon, he was doing a training run. He drove out to a certain area and embarked upon a 10-mile run. He had heard from some not to run at a certain time of day due to packs of dogs roaming the area.

Unfortunately, he did not fully understand the risk and was significantly harmed. Whether it is a walking path or area of potential harm due to animals or ticks, we simply have to take notice.

Population Distribution

Different children do better in different environments. The three main categories regarding population density include urban, suburban, and rural.

My wife and I were counseling a single mom and her sixth-grade son. They lived in a very rural area. He loved to hunt and fish. As well, he was a very good athlete. He was going through a battle due to his dad leaving him and his mom.

The mom liked the city and left the farm house and took her son with her to the city.

I shared that this could be very difficult for her son. Unfortunately, this turned out to be true. He hated the crowds and the lack of space to walk and fish. He went downhill quick. He was not being a baby. He was not trying to cause problems.

They moved back to the farm house and his world changed. He made all those around him proud.

To conclude this chapter, I simply want to reiterate the importance of your need to be proactive as a parent.

It is so easy in today's fast paced world to not take the time to know what truly effects our children positively and negatively. However, when we take the time, it makes all the difference.

Summary

Making a simple composite of primary variables that effect you and your family and keeping it before you may seem unnecessary to some. However, it is very significant in that it enables you to be in control of your circumstance.

This is because when you are aware of specific data regarding the unique makeup of your family and environment you can then live to your highest potential.

Chapter 12

≈⚬≈

A New Day

One of the greatest privileges in life is to be a father or a mother. The intrinsic bond of relationship between a child and their parents is simply amazing. However, there is a lot involved!

As never before in society, there are vehicles of harm that target our children.

Just recently, I became familiar with an app called the stalking app. When given the right information about an individual, it enables you to know their where a bouts at virtually all times. It can show you if they are in their house, and what area in the house they are in! Some say it was invented just for fun but it is not a game.

The vast majority of perpetrators are very intentional and this can be a tool in their hand unto destruction.

The vast majority of time that I am in court helping fight for a young child who is a sexual abuse victim, the perpetrator does not look any different than anyone else.

The majority of time, a man starts out with "regular" porn. Then the website switches the porn to more violent and more abhorrent, all the way down to child porn. It is very prescribed. The visuals are then translated into real life.

Drug dealers are not any different. They are very intentional in their efforts.

They target youth that seem vulnerable. They take them from weed on up. The initial times are always for free.

Most school shooters and sex traffickers have a plan. Consequently, we as parents have to be intentional and have a plan as well.

This book was designed to both help you be proactive and to contribute to your plan. Whether you integrate one wisdom key or 25 of the wisdom keys and principles, it is worth it because our children are worth it.

Herein, I want to encourage you with a few more thoughts.

Courage Needed

Many of the wisdom keys and principles communicated to you are simplistic and rooted in common sense. However, due to these keys and principles being new to many, your interacting with others based on these keys may be more difficult than you think.

For example, your presenting a babysitting application to a prospective babysitter may be seen as you not trusting them. This could become an issue for you with her or her parents that you know.

Likewise, wanting information in regards to a sleep over could be seen as you insinuating that they are not good parents.

I firmly believe in the future, it will be common for parents to utilize babysitting applications, sleep over checklists, even as background checks are in vogue now.

As with virtually all areas of life, such as technology, medicine, and education, safety is progressive in nature.

Case in point, just a decade ago, there was not a zero-tolerance policy regarding bullying. Bullying was seen by many as part of life. Informing a teacher about this type of behavior was even frowned upon. Thankfully, things have drastically changed in this area.

Even today, some of the most basic things that we have highlighted as necessary are looked at as peripheral by many. They are seen as good but not really necessary to the degree that you would risk offending someone or make an extra effort to ensure safety.

Herein, I want to encourage you to be ahead of the curve. I want to encourage you to be ahead of the times. This is a key to safety. Challenges to safety continue to increase. Perpetrators are utilizing technology as never before.

It is imperative that we do not just stick to the status quo. What worked years ago does not necessary work today.

Consequently, it is wisdom to progress in our arsenal of tactics to overcome.

However, it does take an attitude of willingness to see the need and to be courageous to implement what is necessary to ensure our children's safety.

True Relationship – Inside Out

We have shared many things throughout this text, however, it all comes down to relationship. Herein, I want to share one more principle in regard to relationship.

What does it mean to have an inside out relationship with your child as opposed to outside in?

An inside out relationship is heart first. Raising a child is a profound privilege. However, in our busy society where finances necessitate parents working even two jobs, it is easy to interact with our child outwardly.

This does not mean that we do not love our child from the heart. It simply means that due to daily schedule mandates, personality orientation, and sometimes custody arrangements, it is difficult to interact as we would desire.

This is especially true as our children get older and become naturally more and more autonomous. The following are attributes of an inside, heart first relationship.

Outward Second

Every parent wants their child to succeed and rightly so. However, success needs to be defined appropriately regarding a child.

From an early age, children need to be first reinforced in regards to effort rather than by performance. They need to be reinforced regarding who they are as opposed to what they do. Effort will generalize to all areas of life and will bring success.

Believing in Your Child

Children, like it or not will so through stages. As they are establishing their identity, they may say something, or do something derogatory towards you. They may be struggling with their self-concept and fighting depression. There could be a number of challenges that they aren't dealing with appropriately.

The key is to be able to see them as who they really are as opposed to how they are reacting to the various things that they are facing. This does not mean that you dismiss or do not deal with inappropriate behavior. It simply means you deal with things from the inside out.

I have counseled for almost 40 years. It is amazing what believing in your child can do. It is amazing what unconditional love can do.

One parent says, how can you do this to me? How can you struggle like this? How can you be so dumb? You are just like your uncle. You are going to turn out just like him and be in jail.

Another parent states that they believe in their child. They are standing with them. They consistently affirm who they really are in their heart. It makes a profound difference.

No Comparisons

When you parent from the heart, your perception of your child is not based on how he or she compares to others, it is based on who your child is to you. I have shared this at different times in this text due to seeing so many hurt due to comparison and want to share it one more time.

There will always be someone smarter, more athletic, prettier, more handsome, or more successful. Some of the schools with the most successful parents have the highest suicide rates in the nation. This does not mean that parents were not loving or did not put their children first.

However, when very high expectations are coupled with a child's perception that their identity is based on the meeting of these expectations, it can be very difficult for them.

Notice that the word perceived is emphasized in the prior statement.; The parent may not be equating the meeting of expectations with identity. However, if your child perceives it this way, this is reality to them.

First of all, you and your child need to define success. Success is not necessarily what those around you say that success is.

I was just recently talking to a professor and his wife. They were involved in helping host an alumni event. At the event, a commonly asked question was "what do your children do?" Some were doctors, lawyers, and others teachers and nurses. The professor and his wife shared that their son was a mechanic and their daughter a stay at home mom with children.

They were actually looked down upon! I know this couple and their children, they are amazing. They have the most awesome children I have ever met. However, they did not meet the expectations of many of the other parents.

In fact, due to their children's lack of vocational pedigree, they found out that they were not invited to a special gathering of alumni. It is great to be a doctor or a lawyer. It is also great to be a mechanic or a stay at home mom. It is the best to be esteemed for who you are on the inside.

My professor friends did not disclose that their son, the mechanic heroically saved a number of lives while in the army. They also failed to disclose that their daughter had a doctorate in education. They didn't feel the need to.

It is because they had no need to enter into the realm of comparison that was resident. This couple so loved their kids for who they were, they just forgot to mention all that they did.

Again, it is good to set goals and work to meet expectations. This is very significant. However, our children are not employees. They will reach their fullest potential when they are motivated from the inside out.

Enjoying the Process

When you parent from the inside, you will embrace process and true learning. Process involves working through things unto a desired end. In a very busy world with so many demands on us as parents, process can be perceived as both inconvenient and negative.

However, this is what parenting is all about. Together, we work through things with our children. This enables them to get through tough times. It also teaches them how to become solution oriented. As well, it builds a bond between you and your child.

When you parent from the outside in, process can be seen as inconvenient and unnecessary. Simply do not do that again. Life is not perfect, just get over it.

The following are 4 examples of outside parenting as compared to inward parenting.

Hurt by a Friend

Your 7th grade daughter's good friend since 3rd grade distances herself and posts negatively regarding her on Facebook.

Outside in parenting says this. You can never trust people. Tell her off and do not contact her again.

Inside parenting takes time to process with her through sharing and giving insights. Did this just come out of the blue? Did you have an argument just prior to this? Is there anything going on in her life that would cause her to act out of character? What do you think you should do?

Inside parenting does not dictate solutions, but offers possible solutions.

e.g. you have a close mutual friend in "Sue" that might give you insight into what is going on.

e.g. send her a private e-mail sharing of your concern regarding the situation.

e.g. give her a call and ask her to meet you to talk

e.g. let her know that you value her friendship and want to talk.

Process is a process! You then walk with her regarding the responses that she receives. If there is an older sister, perhaps she can share from her experiences as well.

Really Tried and Failed

Your 11th grade son who has his heart set on being a veterinarian is failing at Biology. Outside in parenting says one of the following. It is obvious that you are not trying as hard as you should. Try harder and pass.

If you can't make it, then be honest with yourself and change your expectations regarding your major in college. I have to go work on the car now.

Inward parenting acknowledges that it is very tough class with a very tough teacher. Success in prior science classes is emphasized.

Questions are then asked. Was the subject matter these 9 weeks especially hard? Were the tests especially challenging? What was the average test score?

Possible solutions are then talked about. Would obtaining a tutor possibly help? Julie is in college doing well as a Biology major and she got a C in the class. She had a hard time but it worked out. Would you like to talk to her? Could you do some extra credit work?

Your dad and I know that this is hard for you. Please do not let it define you. Let's take it one day at a time. We both appreciate your hard work and appreciate your fighting spirit.

This type of parenting can make all the difference. This chapter is entitled, *A New Day*. It is closely associated with our last chapter which is called, *Life is to be Good*.

Every day is a new day and every day is to be a good day. Someone may say, with all the evil that is in the world, how can you say that?

It is because when you as a parent live and parent from the heart out, the evil on the outside cannot get in. This is because the inward oriented parent is protected from the outside due to the strength of the heart.

When you pay a price regarding effort and time and believe in your children, they will be committed to their goals and believe in you and what you say.

This is the true foundation of safety. It is not first outward rules, but rules from the heart of relationship.

Struggling with Wrong Friends

Parenting from the outside would deal with this scenario in a very direct manner. These individuals are not good people. Get away from them now.

When parenting from the heart, from the inside out, it is very different. Communication is initiated and questions are asked. Did you feel uncomfortable with this group of students? Why do you think that you started to spend time with them? You can know that you have to break things off completely with them. Will this be hard?

You never know the answers that you will receive until you ask the questions. You never know what is going on. There could be a boy or girl friend involved. There could be gang related activity. There could be a struggle with some type of drugs. It could be a need in the context of identity being formed to want to be with tough kids.

Many times, a child truly wants to be asked what is going on so they can process and receive help. This is why parenting from the inside out can turn a different situation into a true learning experience.

<u>Caught with Marijuana and Pills</u>

Your 17-year-old son, a junior in high school is caught with drugs (Marijuana and pills) in his locker.

Consequently, he is suspended from school for 20 days and will be assigned to alternative class for 20 days. As well, he will not be allowed to participate in basketball his junior year. He was a projected starter.

Mom and dad are surprised by the situation. Dad reacts outwardly and a physical altercation is only avoided due to mom's intervention.

Harsh words are exchanged. Dan conveys his son's actions destroys his reputation in the community. Mom stays quiet. The son struggles and it takes a long time to recover.

The same type of scenario is realized in another family. In this case, the parents react very differently. They ask for the details regarding what was found in his locker. They ask how long he has been involved in using the weed and the pills. They give him opportunity to talk.

In this case, he reverted to the Marijuana and pills when he started to hang around some seniors on the team that he looked up to. His use was infrequent but enough to "fit in".

His parents convey that they believe in him and that they will attend counseling with him. He genuinely apologizes and he is working on weaknesses that led to his wrong decision making. His bond with his parents has become stronger.

The examples given were shared to encourage you to parent from the inside-out, from the heart. It is not just what you do, but how you do it. You can win an argument but lose respect. Your children are looking to you for true love.

Hitting the home run is not the man issue. The key is that you were there to see it. Challenges many times are not what it is always about. It is about seeing that you are there to go through it with them.

Your children need your heart above all. In the midst of their success and their failures, they are looking for your heart response. When they know they have your heart, it enables them to give you theirs.

They are Your Children

This subtitle may seem strange, but in today's society, it is very significant. It is imperative that you understand that there are many who want to put their identity on your children. They include both individuals and institutions.

This is such an important variable, I want to give you a number of real-life scenarios.

There is so much that is involved regarding the area of safety. As well, different challenges regarding safety evolve in society. A decade ago, we would not be talking about cyber bullying, stalking apps, cutting, school shootings, opioid epidemics, child porn, and identity theft as we are now.

Today, there is a prescribed effort by many to superimpose their mindsets upon your children.

This can be done in numerous ways. I am the expert and simply know more than you do regarding how your child should be raised and taught to think. The world has changed and this is the image that all smart children conform to. Culture is meant to bring us all into a unified mindset in that which is most significant.

The bottom line is this, your child is your child he or she is not the property of society as a whole.

Let us look at the following examples in this context.

Dating

Jim and Jane were sweethearts since 6th grade and are happily married with two children. The children are in 6th grade and fifth grade.

Jim and Jane based on their experience initiated a 6th grade prom in their school district. As well, they conveyed their dating experience to their children. As well, they in a very opinionated fashion, conveyed that early dating should be the norm.

Jim and Jane have a right to their opinion. However, they are not your children's parents. Personally, I strongly disagree with their opinion and I have a right to do so.

This was a real-life scenario that parents had to deal with. Unfortunately, many were afraid to express their opinion and some of their children were put into situations they should not have been in.

Again, Jim and Jane have a right to their own opinion, they don't have a right to make decisions regarding your children. So very simply, do not let them!

You would be surprised how others want their mindset to become your mindset.

Marijuana

This text is not to promote one way of thinking above another. Many people feel that Marijuana should be legalized for medical purposes and I agree., others do not. Others believe that Marijuana should be legalized 100% and be available to those at the age of 18. From dealing with those with opioid addictions and being cognizant of addictive personalities in children predispositionally, I do not.

My point is this. Do not let other people or society in general raise your children. You know your children better than anyone. Do not let others determine what you feel is best for your children.

Interestingly enough, a new study has determined when a breast feeding mom smokes Marijuana, the THC chemical (a mind-altering chemical) is found in the baby for up to six days.

Movies

Jill and Jamie are in 8th grade they have been classmates since first grade. They both are invited to go to a sleep over by a girl they have just met. They found out through other peers that certain movies and videos will be shown.

They are very explicit in some ways as well as violent. Jill and Jamie ask their parents for advice and they are told not to go, and they are good with it. Word gets around to both peers and parents. The kids are ostracized to a degree. The parents are called judgmental, intolerant, and moronic! Wow!

Again, people have a right to their opinions, they don't have a right to degrade and harm. In this scenario, what happens all too often is that the parents due to a fear of rejection let other parents make decisions for their children that they are not comfortable with.

The following are two, simple but very significant principles. The individual or institution e.g. school that presents an opinion or concept first to another will usually have the greatest impact upon that individual.

For example, if you as a parent proactively address a subject such as sexuality or opioids prior to one of his peers with a differing view, your impact will be more impactful simply on the basis of initiation.

The second principle involves backing up what you say among others and or in a situation where what you have said is challenged.

For example, if you have taught your son to always respect women and your dad's friend or boss shares a degrading joke against women, in front of him, he is waiting for you to stand up for what you have taught him.

If you do not stand up, the truth you have shared will be minimized, losing its impact. If you do stand up, that which you have shared will be accentuated and grow in its impact.

In essence, your standing up or not standing up will determine who is influencing your child.

Hyperactive Trend

It is amazing how trends affect both individuals and institutions. In our particular school district, I noticed that several parents were told by the Psychologist that their children were hyperactive and had ADD (Attention Deficit Disorder). They were referred to a Psychiatrist that put them on a certain medication.

Now, I believe in labels and in medication. However, I knew these children and, in my opinion, none of them should have been on medication. I shared my opinion with the parents. The Psychiatrist, a good man said that it was possible that the children could make it without meds, but he still felt meds. would be beneficial.

The parents decided to not go with the meds. Their children are at the top of their class. Each of the parents told me after that they did not agree with the recommendation to begin with. They knew their children but thought "who are we to challenge the experts?"

Again, I am not in any way negating the significance of expert opinion. However, as a parent, your opinion is more significant than you know.

Football – to Play, or not to Play

I am very positive towards sports. I played football in high school and coached junior high football when I taught at the high school level.

However, you have to make your own decision regarding your child. I have a friend whose son is very athletic. From first grade, both sets of grand-parents expected this boy to play football. As he got older e.g. 5th grade, his peers and community coaches expected him to play.

Both dad and mom, in the context of concussion research, did not feel good about it. Accordingly, they talked to him and decided against it.

Now this young man was very good in track and cross-country as well as golf. He did participate in these sports.

You would not believe the resistance that they received. The parents and their son made the decision together. With the parents sharing their conclusions from the research they gathered. It was their decision! It was not to be anyone else's decision!

If you feel good about your children playing football or whatever sport, great! If you do not, great!

<u>College</u>

I strongly believe that parenting does not stop when your child enters college. Many times, parenting during these years is more important than at any other time.

Not many years ago, the term "loco parentis" was a key to college administrators. Loco parentis simply means that the college or university would make the school environment commensurate with parental mindset.

However, it is not that way anymore. It seems the exact opposite is true. Many institutions of higher learning have as its objective to conform your child to their mindset. This should be taken into consideration when choosing a school.

I have personally been told by various higher education administrators and professors the following. After four years, our students will become who we want them to be regardless of parental mindset.

I appreciate their honesty and some of these individuals are friends. However, I strongly disagreed with them and will not tell you what I specifically said!

A university did not give birth to my kids, did not raise my kids and are not paying me to send them there.

As well, if they are going to obtain an engineering degree, this is to be the emphasis, not to pressure them into adopting a specific moral mindset.

I counsel college students all the time. Here is a common scenario.

My roommate's boyfriend has basically moved into our room, and they do a lot of weed. I can't stand the smell. I don't want to be mean, but it's my room too! What should I do?? He or she tells me that I am just old fashioned.

Sometimes, it is an easy fix. You can change roommates or get a single room. The key is this. Everyone has a right to their autonomy, to have the right to think like they want. No one has a right to dominate someone else and negate their ability to think for themselves.

They are your children! They are not anyone else's children. Consequently, your input is never to be negated by the undue pressure of someone else.

In today's society, like it or not, our children are targeted by many different types of individuals and institutions to cause them to believe like they do. When younger, they strongly need us as parents to impart structure and identity. As they get older, they still need our input and want it more than we know.

I was counseling a young man recently who signed up for the Army right out of high school. His mom had passed away and his dad was in jail. He is a great young man but was told by his superiors that he would never make it, never be promoted.

We kept in touch a lot. He came so close to quitting. I consistently encouraged him because of his character. To make a long story short, he was recently promoted to Sargent and his future is bright.

One of his new superiors recently, shared that the sky is the limit for him! He thanked me for believing in him. How much more does a parent need to give positive input to their child. Because they are your children, you have both rights and responsibilities that no one else has. You have an ability to know them and strengthen their identity as no one else.

Chapter 13

✂〜✂

Confidence

In our next to last chapter, I want to encourage you. So much of what has been shared is simply to increase your confidence level in the area of safety regarding your children.

Much has been shared in the context of information. It is not meant to overwhelm you but to enable you to implement that which speaks to you most.

Wisdom was emphasized in the context of what challenges that you as a parent face today and how to meet these challenges.

As well, you as an individual was strongly emphasized. This includes your need to be assertive, communicative, consistent in character, and truly knowing your child.

The last variable was especially emphasized in various ways. Again, all of the above, when implemented properly and consistently adhered to translates into confidence.

What you do is incredibly important regarding wisdom. However, how you do it is equally important.

For example, if you tell your daughter or son that you will never tolerate bullying by them and yet you consistently degrade your spouse, your words will not work as you would want.

As well, your confidence level regarding a situation is readily picked up. For example, when you share of zero tolerance regarding underage drinking of alcohol, they can tell to the degree that you really believe it.

One dad shares of zero tolerance in this area but the child knows by his voice that he is doing it to please mom more than anything.

Another dad looks his children right in the eye and speaks boldly with tears, He conveys the necessity of zero tolerance regarding alcohol. He gives examples of harm and leaves no doubt regarding his level of need for them to do right. It makes all the difference.

I shared of the direct correlation between the number of passengers in a vehicle and the number of accidents realized regarding a driver under the age of 23. It is one thing to quote the statistics. It is another thing to see its significance and stand up for it.

I know of school boards that do not act confidently on this reality. They present it as an option due to some parents not wanting the passenger number limited.

In the area of safety, you cannot afford to compromise. Confidence is so important. We have talked much about the importance of positive peer relationship. It is one thing to say that you believe this to be true as well. It is another thing to confidently convey this reality to your children in a very strong way.

Throughout this text, I have given many real-life examples depicting various truths and principles, both positively and negatively. The following is an example of a parent who exemplifies confidence in a profoundly strong way.

This mom was a single mom when I met her, her daughter was 14 years old. She brought her daughter in for counseling due to her skipping school and entering into very harmful peer relationships.

I shared with her but to be honest, she was not very receptive. Her mom was disappointed and then began to cry. After crying deeply, she spoke to her daughter very directly.

She used a very simple analogy. She said, if you hang out with those individuals, you will most likely end up an addict like your aunt and die. It is like you driving down the interstate going 130 miles an hour, you will crash.

Then she said, if you choose to have friends like you once hung out with, you will live the way you know that you should and you will help so many others. Then she concluded by saying, "life and death are really before you. Then she began to weep again and embraced her.

I knew the peers and they were peers of harm. The mom was so right, they were older and all involved with Heroin. Surprisingly, the daughter did not initially respond. Then the mom reiterated her love for her and wept again. It was then that her daughter responded by simply saying Ok. I then shared some ways for her to be assertive and the three of us talked for a while. Her attitude was very different than when she came in. This young girl chose life and is now in college majoring in social work. She is amazing.

I have never seen any parent convey un-hesitantly, ultra-confidently speak in the way she did. It wasn't like, maybe these kids and you will be ok. It wasn't, I feel like you are going over the speed limit and could get hurt. She was so confident in the validity of peer influence specific to those that she was gravitating to, she spoke in a way that only she could as a mom. She spoke with a confidence that conveyed definite, now reality.

This is how we are to live. This is how we are to parent. We are to parent both confidently and passionately.

Confident parenting in regard to safety does not mean that our children will never scrape their knee. It does not mean that they will never go through stages that are challenging or never make wrong decisions.

It does not mean that we minimize various problems, but that we always provide safety and strength as we are able. It means that we can see the light at the end of the challenge and convey that hope when our children don't seem to have it.

Safety is not just keeping them out of harm. It is also providing a safety net when they unexpectedly fall. You are never going to be perfect and neither are they. However, when you are doing the best that you can, this is what makes you the best parent that your child can have.

Children know when you are giving them your best. Intrinsically, they will respond by giving you their best. They will grow in confidence themselves. Even as you are motivated to do all that you can to keep them safe due to your love for them, it will produce a like motivation in them.

They will be motivated to make right decisions resulting in safety because they want to respond as they have been taught. It is a cycle that relationship thrives on.

Chapter 14

Life is to be Good

Children are an amazing gift. The belly laugh of an infant conveys a joy and a hope within that cannot be measured. The smile of accomplishment and the tears of difficulty, both penetrate you as a parent equally.

Safety is not just a responsibility and an objective, it is a parental privilege. I do not know what you expected when you started to read this text, perhaps you did not expect it to be so encompassing, thinking that it would just deal with physical safety.

I have accentuated emotional safety, the affective domain alongside the variable of physical safety. This is for two reasons. The first is that the root of physical safety is relationship. Your children will only listen to you and value your instruction to the degree that they know that you value them.

Second, in today's society, there is as assault not only in the context of physical harm e.g. school shootings but in the context of negating the influence of parents to superimpose their mindsets on our children.

This is why it is so important for there to be communication and an emotional connection with our children as well. If we do not communicate and establish strong emotional ties with our children, there will be a void that is resident.

Herein, the void will be filled by others in a very harmful manner through internet relationships, and harmful types of social media. Our children are now targeted in this manner, like never before. The key way to combat this reality is safety through relationship. It is a reality where there are no voids.

A while ago, I was working with a very good foster care agency. They referred a 16-year-old girl to us who was waiting for a family. She was in a group home.

There was a family with a 19-year-old daughter that was finishing her freshman year at a nearby college who was a social work major.

The family of the girl that was mentoring, was also involved. When meeting with the mentor, she shared something that I never forgot. She shared that it took a while for "Sally" (the girl from the group home) to begin to feel comfortable with her and her family.

Sally asked two questions. Why does your mom always want to know all about your day? Isn't that annoying. Sarah, the mentor, replied by saying no. That is just what mom's do. It shows that she cares. While Sally was with Sarah in the car, Sarah backed into the mailbox and put a dent in the car. Sarah's dad came out and treated her with kindness. He was very forgiving and consoled her regarding this mistake.

Sally asked Sarah "how could your dad not be upset at you and yell at you for what you did? Sarah's response was as follows. That's just what dad's do.

After a few months, Sally began to change. When asked what she wanted most regarding foster parents, she said the following. I want a dad and mom who do what dad's and mom's do.

There is a lot of pressure on mom's and dad's today. There are personal issues. There are interpersonal challenges. There are financial challenges. Most of all, there is the development of our children and that includes definite challenges.

However, even as Sally's greatest desire was to have parents that unselfishly would love her, the heart of a parent is to lay their life down for their children.

I know this is the reason you are reading this text. You want the best for your children.

In summary, my greatest desire is for you to enjoy life and at the same time enjoy your responsibility as a parent regarding safety. To do this, you have to know that what you do in regard to safety may entail work, but it is so worth it.

You would not go on a diet if you did not believe that you would lose weight. You would not invest in the stock market if you did not believe that it would pay dividends.

However, if you know that if you invest time and energy unto a desired end, you will do it. Herein, when you know that if you pay a price in regard to your child's safety, that it will benefit them, you will certainly do it.

As we conclude our time together regarding this text, I simply want to share two more scenarios with you that accentuate your significance as a decision maker. Then I want to share with you a few concluding thoughts from my heart.

Red Flags

We have talked a lot about red flags. Your child is feeling depressed. They are spending a tremendous amount of time with video games that are violent.

Your teenage daughter is hesitant to go to piano lessons with a well-known music teacher. She is there for the lesson and it seems that his wife and kids are not around during the lesson.

Again, you are so busy. You are a trusting person who does not like conflict with your children or anyone else. This is not the core issue. The primary issue is if you will step out of your comfort zone and investigate what these red flags may be indicative of. I believe that you will.

Cars, Ticks, Bridges, and Chaperones

I had a single mom come to me recently. Her son had just completed 10th grade and is very popular in school.

He is invited by a friend on the baseball team to join four other guys on the team to spend the weekend at his father's camp.

I asked her why she was concerned, she shared the following. The friend driving has a bad reputation regarding driving, always going too fast. This boy and his brother both contracted Lyme's disease from ticks at the camp. She overheard the boy's talking about diving off a railroad bridge. The friend's dad who owned the camp, the primary chaperone was known for letting his teenage children drink.

Before I could share the obvious, she said this: I will tell his friend not to drive too fast. I will give my son spray that will take care of ticks. When I was my son's age, I jumped off a bridge like that one and I am fine. My dad is friends with the owner of the camp.

Wow. I looked her right in the eye and shared that she was using the word but to make excuses that would negate the truth of the situation that would put her son in danger.

I know that he drives fast, but it will be alright. I know that he has two friends who talk about porn, but boys will be boys. I know that my daughter felt uncomfortable when the voice coach put his hand on her arm, but he has a good reputation.

The list goes on and on. Literally, when you utilize the word but as in the above statements, it excludes all that comes before it.

In this case with the single mom, I went over each of her statements logically negating the buts.

This boy is not going to obey your request to drive the speed limit. These young people will drink and he will drive while under the influence and you know it. What happens if they drink and then jump off the bridge while intoxicated? Do you even know how high the bridge is and how deep the water level is?

It turned out that she did not want to have a confrontation with her dad who was friends with the father and owner of the camp, relationship was already strained and he would not understand.

However, after our session, she decided to not allow her son to go to the camp. He actually told his mom that he really did not want to go and was very glad for her decision. He shared of not wanting to be in that environment and especially not wanting to dive off the bridge.

We are all human. As a result, things are easier said than done at times. However, I believe that your love for your children and the need for their safety will enable you to do that which is necessary for them.

Now, I simply want to share 5 things as this text concludes.

First, I want to thank you for your desire to keep your children safe and for your commitment therein.

Second, I want to say this to those who may never have heard about some of the solutions presented and have experienced pain or loss.

I constantly have parents come up and say that they wish they had heard of what they were up against and how to deal with different situations prior. You are not to feel condemned, you are to know that people respect you for having done the best that you knew to do.

Third, do not be intimidated by that which you cannot control regarding society as a whole. Work on what you can control regarding your own children and those closest to you.

Fourth, you may not be able to change everything but think Big! You may have the answer or can form a task team to finding solutions that nobody has had solutions for prior. It may be a safer car seat or a national organization helping children whose parents struggle with addictions. It may be teaching new moms who don't have parents about safety. Do not limit yourself!

Lastly, in the eyes of your child, you are the best mom and dad, grandma and grandpap that there is. They learn to trust through your love and wisdom. They then become trustworthy themselves.

In a world where we are trying to find those who we can trust, it is so good to know that your children will be those that are trustworthy because of you!

Evaluations
and
Babysitting Application

DAYCARE EVALUATION

Interview Questions:

1. What certifications do you have as a center?

2. Do all workers have clearances?

3. What are the credentials of your teachers?

4. Is your building up to all current safety codes?

5. What is the teacher-student ratio?

6. If a child causes other children to be physically at risk, what is your due process regarding this child?

7. What forms of discipline do you utilize? e.g. time out

8. Could I see your references?

9. Are toys sanitized daily?

10. How do you keep unwanted visitors out of your building?

11. Do you have cameras on site?

12. Do you give daily reports of my child's interaction and progress?

Sleepover Evaluation

1. Who will be the primary chaperones at the sleepover?

2. Will anyone else be in the house during the sleepover and if so, who?

3. Does/did anyone involved in chaperoning or in the house had/ have any addiction problems or criminal record?

4. How many individuals will be present?

5. What types of activities will be presented during the sleepover?

6. Will the participants ever leave the house during the sleepover to go somewhere else?

7. Are there any animals that will be present?

8. Does your child express any apprehension concerning the sleepover?

9. Do you know other parents who have had their child participate in an overnight stay at this residence?

10. How well does your child know those participating in the sleep over?

Peer Evaluation

- What is the age of the individual that you are considering to become your friend?

- How did you meet that individual?

- What type of reputation do they have regarding morality?

- Have they ever had any type of drug involvement?

- What are their 3 main interests?

- What is their GPA academically?

- Why do you want to have this individual as a friend?

- What do you feel the 3 main strengths of this person are?

- Who do you feel are the main friends that this individual has?

- Does this individual have any anger issues?

- Is their outlook mostly positive or negative?

- What is the individuals attitude like toward authority figures?

- What are the future plans of this individual?

- Can this person take constructive criticism in a good way?

- Does this individual treat persons of the opposite sex with respect?

- Are there any racial or prejudice types of attitudes in this individual?

- What do you think are the 3 main adjectives that the individual would use to describe themselves?

- What are the 3 main adjectives that others would use to describe this individual?

- Would this person be considered a giver, a taker or in-between?

Babysitting Application

Name: _____

Address: _____

_____

_____

_____

Phone: _____

E-mail: _____

Age: _____

Babysitting Certification(s): _____

_____

_____

_____

Babysitting Experience: _____

_____

_____

_____

_____

Please list 3 references: _____

_____

_____

_____

_____

_____

_____

_____

Please answer the following questions as honestly as you can:

1. What ages do you enjoy working with most?

2. What do you feel are your greatest strengths are regarding babysitting?

3. What do you feel are your greatest weaknesses regarding babysitting?

4. If a child continues to cry and cry, would it upset you?

5. If a child continued to cry and cry what would you do?

6. What do you like most about babysitting?

7. Have you ever had a bad experience babysitting? Please explain.

8. Would it bother you if there were cameras in the house?

9. Who is someone that you esteem highly?

10. Would you share 3 words that you feel describe you the best.

Scenarios:

*If you are babysitting and someone that you know shows up at the door unexpectedly that you were not to let in, what would you do?

*If you were having a bad day and then the children were not being good, how would this effect you? Please explain.

*If the children were playing in the yard and would not come inside when you asked them to, what would you do?

*If you were asked not to use your cell phone during babysitting time and you know a friend was having a hard time due to breaking up with her boyfriend, would it be hard not to turn your phone on?

*Do you feel that having to fill out this babysitting form is a positive or negative thing? Please explain.

About the Author

Michael Bruno is the founder and director of Abba Ministries Counseling Center. He has been involved in the counseling field relative to safety for almost 40 years.

This includes the areas of sexual abuse, bullying, opioid addiction, and general child development issues.

After receiving an undergraduate degree in education, master's degree in Psychology and doing post masters work in administration, he taught and coached at the high school level for six years.

He also has served on his local school board and was chairman of the safety committee.

He and his wife Kathy have raised four children and now have three grandchildren.

He was a forerunner 40 years ago regarding the area of sexual abuse when few wanted to recognize it as a problem. The programs devised by Michael Bruno regarding sexual abuse, and bullying have over a 95% success rate.

His hope and passion is to enable every parent or caregiver to proactively and confidently raise their children in safety in a world that is becoming increasingly unsafe. It is also to encourage parents to utilize their skills and creativity to help all children in society to be able to be nurtured in a safe environment.

www.ingramcontent.com/pod-product-compliance
Lightning Source LLC
LaVergne TN
LVHW051502080426
835509LV00017B/1886